CHESH

R. N. Dore

CHESHIRE

B. T. Batsford
London

AUTHOR'S NOTE

Change has been one of the main themes of this book and it has not ceased to operate even in the short period of time since the text was completed. So that a few of the statements made there are already out of date. In Chester itself the High Cross has been restored to its rightful place in the centre of the town (see the photograph on p. 18); the museum of the Cheshire Regiment has found roomier quarters in the great court of Chester castle; the Grosvenor Museum has been modified to give more prominence to post-Roman antiquities.

First published 1977·
Copyright R. N. Dore 1977
Printed in Great Britain by
The Pitman Press Ltd, Bath
for the Publishers B. T. Batsford Ltd
4 Fitzhardinge Street, London W1H 0AH

ISBN 0 7134 3187 3

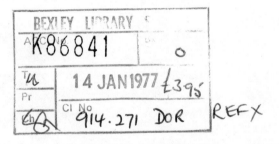

Contents

Acknowledgments

Far too many people and organisations have given me assistance in the compilation of this book for me to acknowledge them all by name, but I would like to make an exception in the case of the staff of the Altrincham Library. The facilities they have given me for consulting their excellent collection of printed books on Cheshire history have made the task of collating and checking my information infinitely easier.

I would also like to thank the following for their permission to reproduce the photographs in this book: J. Allan Cash Ltd, nos 1, 13; A. F. Kersting, nos 5, 7, 8, 9, 10, 11, 16, 18, 19, 24; Kenneth Scowen, no. 4; Vernon Shaw, nos. 2, 3, 6, 12, 14, 15, 20, 25, 26, 27; S. C. Sedgwick, no. 17. Nos 21, 22 and 23 are the property of the publishers.

List of Illustrations

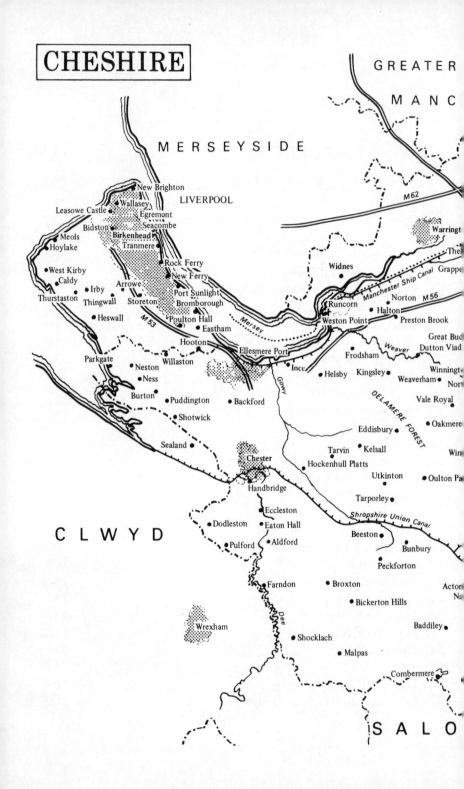

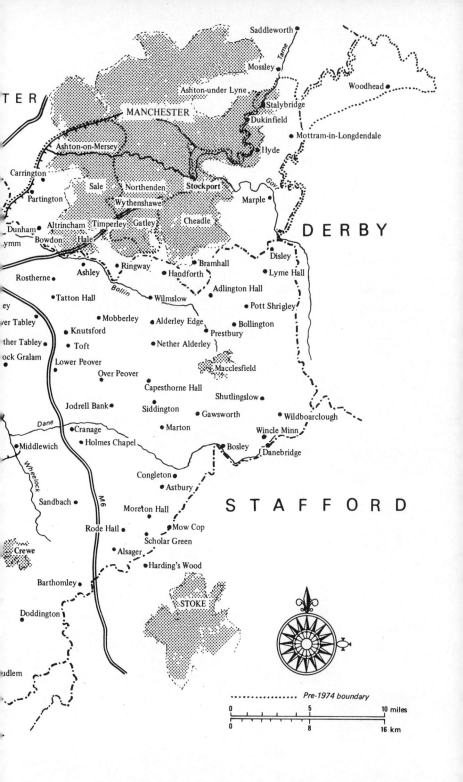

To my wife, who has suffered much in the cause of Local History, but thoroughly approved and appreciated the making of this one.

Introduction

'And the next year *Chestershire* was ravaged by the Norsemen.'

This entry from the *Anglo-Saxon Chronicle* for the year A.D. 980 first
tells us that Cheshire was in existence. Unlike many of the counties in the
south and east, it was not shaped by the settlement of one tribe or folk.
We do not know what Celtic tribe occupied its area at the time of the
Roman Conquest. If the origins of the place-names Tarvin (Welsh *terfyn*,
a boundary) and Macefen by Malpas (Welsh *maes-y-ffin*, the boundary
field) have any significance, then it would seem to have been divided
between two or more Celtic princedoms after Roman rule had ended. It
was a Northumbrian king who first pushed forward and won a great
victory against the Celtic princes near Chester round about A.D. 616.
Yet the first Saxon settlers seem to have come more from Mercia than
Northumbria.

None of these circumstances brought about the formation of Cheshire,
which resulted from the later struggle of the Saxon kingdom of Wessex
against the Norsemen. Alfred's men drove from Chester a roving band of
Vikings who had occupied it. His son and successor, Edward, and his
warrior daughter, Ethelfleda, wife to the invalid ealdorman of Mercia,
fortified and re-garrisoned the old Roman fortress and built new *burhs* at
Eddisbury, Runcorn and Thelwall. The area was invaluable as a wedge
driven into the communication lines between Norsemen established at
York and at Dublin. It may well have been at Bromborough in the Wirral
that Alfred's grandsons, Athelstan and Edmund, broke the coalition
between such Norsemen and the Scots formed to halt the progress of

Wessex and, by their victory, made certain a Saxon kingdom of all
England. The site of the great battle of Brunanburh, fought in 937, is no
longer known, but etymologically Bromborough is an allowable
candidate and geographically a probable one. What is more certain is that
Edgar, Alfred's great grandson and the first accepted king of England,
after he had been crowned in Bath in 973, brought his fleet to Chester
and there received an acknowledgment of his supremacy from the other
princes of Britain. At some time during this march of events Cheshire
must have been formed and proclaimed.

It is quite clear that the new shire was, in fact as well as in name,
hester—shire; brought into existence because of Roman *Deva* and
formed around it. Whether or not long periods of decay had come to the
fortress town after the Romans left, it was the one place known outside
the region and capable, because of its position and its traditions, of
becoming again a great centre. Until the late eighteenth century no other
Cheshire town surpassed it in size, and none has ever come near it in fame
or attractiveness to those outside the county.

In the Middle Ages Cheshire became a County Palatine. If continental
precedents were followed, this should have meant that it was a kind of
semi-independent principality and that its earl enjoyed powers which
elsewhere belonged to the king alone. Whether this was really so has been
a matter of controversy among scholars for many years. Over twenty
years ago Professor Barraclough poured a cold douche upon the pride of
local historians in their county's great past by pointing out that the term
County Palatine as applied to Cheshire does not appear in any record until
the Crown had taken the earldom over and that, therefore, it might well
be no more than an empty title. In addition, the famous Norman earls of
Chester had all owned vast lands elsewhere, both in England and in
Normandy, and it was these, and not their poverty-stricken little county
in the north-west, which made them of such account in the kingdom.
Barraclough's scholarship was such that, after the protests had died down,
his views were generally accepted, but now voices are being heard to say
that they went too far, and that even if Cheshire was not *called* a County
Palatine, there is plenty of evidence that, in the days of Hugh Lupus,
Ranulf II and Ranulf III, it did have a considerable measure of
independence. Cheshire barons did get their own charter from Ranulf III
at the same time as the English barons forced John to grant Magna Carta.

The terms of military service for Cheshire knights were not the same as for knights elsewhere in the kingdom. The county did have a different financial system and some administrative and judicial institutions different from the rest of England. These views are likely to find expression in the forthcoming and long-awaited *Victoria County History of Cheshire*.

The main purpose of these special powers was obviously to enable the county to deal with the warlike and restless princes of North Wales at times when the king and the rest of the nation were occupied elsewhere. Chester was the base and the Cheshire forces the spearhead of Edward I's conquest of Wales from 1277-83. Yet this conquest, as much as the taking over of the earldom by the king after the failure of the line of the Norman earls, was the cause of the decline of the county's military importance and, with it, its semi-independence. For a century after the end of the Welsh wars the old military tradition made Cheshire knights and Cheshire archers outstanding in service in the Hundred Years War. But Richard II's attempt to make the county's soldiers the basis for strong rule over the rest of the country was a dismal failure, and they played no outstanding part in the Wars of the Roses.

Under the Tudor and Stuart monarchs Cheshire regained some national importance in the long struggle to subjugate Ireland. But this was rather because Chester was the main port for the embarkation of troops and supplies for Ireland, while its gentry provided many of the royal officials there, than because the manpower and resources of the whole county were employed in it. The Civil War brought a struggle between the opposing parties in Cheshire and Lancashire as prolonged and bitter as any in the country, but it was always something of a side-show. No major battles were fought in or near the county, and it was only later that the soldiers of Sir William Brereton, the parliamentary commander, saw wider service as additional regiments of the New Model Army.

There is no doubt that by this time the county was notable in the eyes of those living outside it, not for its military prowess nor for its palatine status which had become no more than a name, but for its *cheese*. As John Speed said:

'The soil is fat fruitful and rich ... the Pastures make the Kine's udders to strout to the pail, from whom and wherein the best Cheese of all Europe is made.'

The cool, moist summers and the blanket of clay, hitherto discouraging to farmers wanting tillage above everything else, were becoming the county's greatest assets. Every wide-awake traveller who now came to it looked on every side for signs of cheese production. Celia Fiennes, the intrepid lady who traversed England from end to end in the reign of William III with no more than a couple of servants for company, was disappointed that she did not see vast herds of cattle browsing on its pastures. Defoe believed the most ludicrously high figures given him for the tonnage of Cheshire cheese despatched to London annually. John Byng, ex-officer of the Guards and lofty aristocrat, in 1790 and George Borrow, pugnacious individualist, in 1854 expected a very special treat when they ordered cheese in Cheshire pubs. Both were horribly disappointed (this can happen today) and concluded that all the real Cheshire cheese was sent to London.

Cheshire continued to be a great cheese-producing county until recent times and Cheshire cheese is still noted far and wide. Indeed I have met several (and some even in the county itself) who were convinced that the derivation of the word Cheshire itself was *cheese-shire*. Modern transport and methods of preservation, however, have brought in rival cheeses from abroad and concentrated the making of Cheshire cheese in creameries. There are several of these in southern Cheshire, but not many more than a dozen farms in the county that continue to make cheese. But the production of milk has continued, so that herds of cows are still a common sight in Cheshire fields. Just after the Second World War it was said to be the most densely stocked dairy cattle area in the whole world, and it still has around about 140,000 dairy cows and produces 120,000,000 gallons of milk a day.

Although Cheshire developed considerable industries of her own which owed nothing to Lancashire, such as silk in Macclesfield and Congleton and salt and chemicals in mid-Cheshire, the Industrial Revolution had the effect of putting Cheshire very much under the shadow of a Lancashire which had developed suddenly from a sparsely populated and backward region into one of the country's great centres of industry. A whole area of north-east Cheshire became an extension of Lancashire's cotton field, the border between the counties virtually disappearing in the process. With a few exceptions the tremendous network of communications by road, canal and rail, which grew up in Cheshire, was put there to link southern

Lancashire surely and speedily to Liverpool, to the great industrial area of the Midlands and to London. Market gardening sprouted all over northern Cheshire primarily to feed the towns of southern Lancashire. Finally, when more and more railway lines pushed south and more and more steam ferry services crossed the Mersey, more and more Lancashire people began to use Cheshire for their recreation and, if they were wealthy enough, for their homes.

This intermingling, not so much of two different counties as of two different societies, was not without its strains and stresses. Cheshire farmers and cottagers, although they often made some money out of it, did not always appreciate the trippers who flooded out to their quiet villages in search of noisy entertainment. (The village festivities which Rowland Egerton-Warburton, the 'Merrie England' squire, had revived at Arley Green, had to be abandoned because of visitors from Manchester. 'Merriness' could be taken too far.) The Cheshire squires of ancient descent despised the society of the wealthy manufacturers and merchants who bought villas at Alderley Edge and Bowdon. In return, it must be said that most of the families of the merchants and manufacturers did not attempt to imitate the county gentry or claim acquaintance with them and regarded such of their kind as did with scorn.

Despite this, there were (and still are) accusations from those who have stayed north of the Mersey, either because they preferred to or because they could not afford to move across it, that those who did were too proud to live in the place that their money came from and were turning into southern snobs. It is mostly from Lancashire folk or from those of other industrial areas of the North that talk comes of Cheshire's 'swell-belt', of the 'Surrey of the North' or – more recently and snidely – of 'a little piece of Surrey that got lost along the M6'. Your true Londoner or Home Counties man would never believe there could be a 'Surrey' in the North. In fact, since the decline of Britain's old heavy industry with its dependence on coal, the pattern has been changing. Much light industry has spread across Cheshire, and a whole new area of refineries and factories has sprung up at Ellesmere Port and Stanlow which, although originally created by the existence of the Manchester Ship Canal, is not dependent on Manchester and south Lancashire. With this the pattern of commuting has altered also, a great many people commuting from one part of Cheshire to another. Even before the recent local government changes, 75% of the working population of the county was employed within its boundaries.

These developments came too late to prevent the submerging of much that was characteristic of the old Cheshire. The first stage of the Industrial Revolution had added to the population, but mostly through the increase of those already in the county, with some additions from just over its borders. The speed-up of communications by the spread of railways opened the floodgates. This was expressed by Sir John Brunner, one of the two founders of Brunner Mond's alkali works at Northwich, in answer to a heckler during an election campaign in the 1880s. 'My father was Swiss, my mother was a Manxwoman, I was born in Liverpool, my nurse was Welsh. Is that Cheshire enough for you?' Round about this time folk-speech students were busy collecting and publishing Cheshire dialect words. They filled whole books with them, but hardly any are in use now, and it is scarcely possible to distinguish a Cheshire accent.

There has followed the inevitable dismemberment of the old county. It began in a small way with the creation of county boroughs at the end of the last century. But Cheshire county boroughs were few in number and comparatively small: Stockport and Birkenhead, the largest of them, have populations of little more than 140,000. Then, in the period between the World Wars, Manchester pushed not just her commuters but her city government south of the Mersey to Northenden and Wythenshawe. It was the commuter areas, however, which brought about the final dismemberment. As their inhabitants worked mostly in Liverpool or Manchester, which they could reach in about 30 minutes, so more and more of the essential services were provided from these towns. Direction from Chester, which otherwise played no part in their lives, over matters of education, police and local taxation became more and more of an anomaly. In the local government changes of 1974, these areas were transferred to the new Metropolitan authorities of Greater Manchester and Merseyside.

Cheshire survived and, indeed, had a section of old Lancashire, Warrington and Widnes and the districts around them, added to it. (In the original Redcliffe-Maud local government reform proposals, it was to have disappeared altogether, divided up between urban authorities in Manchester, Liverpool and Stoke.) But its old shape, which excited the

1　The Eastgate, Chester: clock of 1897 over the eighteenth-century gateway.

comments of the Tudor topographers and made a very distinctive outline on the map has been destroyed. What made it unusual was the Wirral and the narrow north-eastern arm thrust in between Lancashire, Derbyshire and Yorkshire. William Webb, who wrote a perambulation of the county in the 1620s which was later published in *King's Vale-Royall of England* in 1656, likened the whole outline of the county to an eagle's wing outstretched and the north-eastern projection to 'the point of the wing's first feather reaching forth beyond all the rest'. This metaphor, taken from the eagle of heraldry rather than the actual bird, would have been appreciated by the lineage-conscious gentry for whom he wrote, but when thousands of working class people began to inhabit the area, the homelier epithet of the 'Panhandle' was substituted. By this time tea had become the national beverage and late nineteenth-century writers found in the humble teapot the most accurate image for portraying Cheshire's shape. The Wirral was the spout, the north-eastern arm the handle, the Staffordshire border the bottom and the curve of the Mersey from Warrington to Northenden the lid. Handle and spout have now been broken off and the lid removed, and the amorphous and irregular outline of the new county is unlikely to exercise the ingenuity of future topographers.

The old outline was, in fact, not just an intriguing line on the map. Before modern means of communications eliminated some of it, it had geographical reality. The whole of the Mersey, with its attendant marshes and peat bogs, was a considerable barrier until medieval times; its estuary remained one until the steam ferries came. The Shropshire moraine seems to us hardly an obstacle at all. Yet the Norman-French name *Malpas* and its Saxon predecessor *Depenbech* both refer to a difficult passage, so in those times it cannot have been negligible. The Pennines still cause trouble in winter, and the lack of bridges across the Dee above Chester can, at the very least, be a nuisance to the traveller. Enclosed in these natural boundaries was a great plain, not very level, it is true, and in its centre rising to rounded highlands, but nowhere uncrossable even in primitive times. These boundaries would once have had military significance and it is probable that they were the basic limits of Cheshire from its very beginning. The Welsh border, it is true, swayed back and forwards across the Dee, because of the varying fortunes and complications of war between the Welsh and the English, as the later chapter on Cheshire's

2 above *The High Cross, recently restored at the centre of the Rows, Chester.* 3 below *Boathouses beside the Dee at Chester; in the background is the suspension footbridge linking Grosvenor and Queen's Parks.*

Welsh border will show. Yet the Dee was a constant factor to which the exhausted combatants tended to revert. The inclusion of the manors of southern Lancashire at the end of the entry for Cheshire in the Domesday Book has caused some to think that this area was part of Cheshire at the time, but there is stronger evidence from the *Anglo-Saxon Chronicle* that the Mersey was the northern boundary of the county, at any rate at the time of its origin. It is the Mersey boundary which has now been totally obliterated. This is only the final conclusion of a process of eliminating it as a natural obstacle which has covered many centuries. Medieval bridges of timber and stone began it; nineteenth- and twentieth-century bridges of every type – high level, swing, transporter and suspension – viaducts and tunnels have completed it. Now Merseyside and Greater Manchester flow across it southwards and Cheshire itself northwards.

For the purposes of this book I have kept to the 'teapot', the old basic boundaries. In talking about what has happened in an area over the long centuries: what has developed into that which we see today, what has gone but left relics, what has disappeared utterly, one cannot adopt a framework invented yesterday.

Apart from Chester itself, Cheshire has not attracted a great number of visitors in modern times. Probably the feeling that it is only a threshold to Lancashire without the true Lancashire flavour has had its effect. For the true industrial scene, it is said, one should go to Lancashire. If one wants to avoid it, it is better to go further afield. As for suburbia, who wants to visit that? And yet Cheshire has a great deal to offer. Probably no county in England has greater variations of climate and natural scenery. The eastern border is wet and wild; the Wirral as mild and sunny as many parts of eastern and southern England. There are great moors, a stretch of sea coast (albeit somewhat tamed and urbanised), two very different estuaries, forest and pleasant rolling uplands, many meres with fascinating wild life, miles and miles of twisting country roads running through woods and meadows and passing little hamlets, old churches and halls and farmhouses. Nor is its modern urban development without interest, even its miles of suburbia. I have done no justice at all to the wealth of Victoriana in the county. For a small book there is just too much of it at the moment. Furthermore, almost all Victorian houses are privately owned and very much lived in, and Victorian churches, being mostly town churches, are usually locked. (It used to be the assumption that country churches would not be. Unfortunately with the spread of vandalism, this is no longer true.) But many of the great Victorian architects — Blore, Salvin, Butterfield, Bodley, Blomfield — designed buildings in the county, while there is a great deal of the work of George Gilbert Scott and the famous partners, Austin and Paley. There was also a good Cheshire-born architect, John Douglas. For details of the sites, styles and architects of these buildings, the reader is referred to the *Cheshire* volume by Pevsner and Hubbard in the *Buildings of England* series.

I have not been able to do much more than mention outstanding twentieth-century building developments. Certain types of these would, on a county-wide scale, make a fascinating study. In the last 20 years civic centres and shopping precincts, sometimes separate, sometimes combined, have appeared everywhere, from the Mersey to the south-east gateway, from the Wirral to the 'Panhandle'. Few are likely to meet with total approbation, and the traditionalist will probably condemn the lot. Nevertheless they represent an attempt to find an answer to some of our needs and problems, just as the nineteenth-century railways, viaducts and town halls, the eighteenth-century canal embankments and turnpike roads, the Tudor half-timbered halls and cottages, the medieval churches and monasteries were the answers which former communities found for some of theirs. Ingenuity has gone into the making of many of them, and some reflect well enough the new prosperity and pride of those who had them built.

ONE

Chester

Outside the magic triangle of London, Stratford and Oxford, no place in Britain has been more visited and patronised by Americans than Chester. Until quite recently they entered this country through Liverpool and close at hand was what they desired to see. Nathaniel Hawthorne, consul at Liverpool from 1853-57, was one of many famous American writers to visit Chester: 'It is a quite indescribable old town; and I feel, at last, as if I had had a glimpse of Old England.'

80 years later a noted English travel writer, H. V. Morton, was even more categorical about its ancientry: 'Chester is as "medieval" as Clovelly is "quaint". There is no getting away from it.' And yet now, in our own day and age, Pevsner and Hubbard have declared, 'Chester is not a medieval city, it is a Victorian one ... 95% is Victorian and after.' That they are referring to the 'old' centre is obvious. For if suburbs are included, no existing British town could be other than '95% Victorian and after'; furthermore they follow up their challenging statement by a detailed examination of all the buildings in or near the famous Rows. They are able to show that the greater part of the black and white, apparently timber-framed, houses of this area are the work of T. M. Penson, T. M. Lockwood and John Douglas, executed between the late 1850s and 1900. The timberwork is mostly a façade nailed on to brick walls, but with the black and white Tudor and Jacobean motives so cunningly imitated and adapted that they can deceive all but the expert. Hawthorne was in Chester before they were built, but they certainly took in Morton. Nowadays this style of building is no longer dismissed out of hand as 'pseudo' or 'stockbrokers' Tudor' (stockbrokers have never

played much part in the making of Chester), and is taken quite seriously by students of architecture. It is possible, therefore, to put old prejudices aside and admire the richness and exuberance of the south side of Eastgate Street from Douglas's delightful Diamond Jubilee Clock on the Gate itself to Lockwood's turreted and many-gabled block at the junction with Bridge Street.

Nevertheless, when all this has been taken into consideration, the statement that Chester is a Victorian city is misleading, and anyone who cares to compare Chester to Manchester can see why. Manchester is almost as old as Chester in its origin and not without relics of its distant past. Yet they are no more than relics, and the layout and atmosphere of modern Manchester owes hardly anything to that past. The centre of Manchester is Albert Square with its Albert Memorial, its statues of Victorian worthies and its great Victorian town hall. All emphasise that these were the days of Manchester's greatness and that the more distant past was comparatively unimportant. It is very different in the centre of Chester.

Here, through the recent passing of some sensible and imaginative traffic regulations, the visitor can walk in a little strip of ground no more than 50 yards long which stretches from the junction of Bridge Street and Watergate Street to the junction of Eastgate Street and Northgate Street. It is where the High Cross once stood. The line of these streets has been altered not at all since Tudor times and, with the exception of the southern half of the Northgate, not very much since the days of the Roman fortress. If the visitor faces north he will be looking at St Peter's church. It is a church much restored throughout the centuries, the seventeenth, eighteenth and even the twentieth century playing their part as well as the Victorians. Yet its core is late medieval, and at that time and later it was the principal church for the mayor and corporation, and their government was conducted in a wooden building attached to it called the 'Pentice'. There was a church on the site when Domesday Survey was made. Under it and the buildings behind it lay in Roman times the *principium,* the legionary headquarters, and behind that again the *praetoria,* the residence of the commanding officer. Some of the bases of the columns of the hall of the *principium* still stand in the cellars of a modern shop in Northgate Street.

Eastgate Street is almost wholly Victorian and there is much Victorian restoration in Watergate Street. But under Brown's, the most famous of all Chester shops, is a fine rib-vaulted medieval crypt of four bays. There are a dozen or so more medieval crypts and cellars, most of them under the shops of Watergate Street. Here, where the Rows are continuous on both sides almost to Nicholas Street, are the 'long tunnels . . . almost pitch black', which H. V. Morton found so eerie at night time, 'half-expecting to hear the scuffle of hired assassins and the gasp of a man with a dagger in his neck'. The atmosphere is certainly more Tudor than nineteenth-century.

At the end of these four streets are the city walls. They have a circumference of nearly two miles and are the only complete ones in England, although in the south-west they are not much more than a token, being incorporated into roadways and the banks of the Dee. The four principal gates were rebuilt in the late eighteenth century and the Newgate (south of the Eastgate) is a twentieth-century reproduction of a Roman gateway which certainly never existed in that position in Deva. The triangular coping outside the parapet walk was put in instead of the old crenellation in the days after the Civil War, when the citizens began to appreciate their walls as an unusual and pleasant promenade and not any longer as a safeguard against an enemy. The foundations of the walls, however, are Roman for the northern two-thirds of the east wall and the eastern two-thirds of the north wall, and early medieval for the rest. It is interesting to note that Chester citizens and lovers of Chester received an earlier jolt from the experts over the question of the age of the walls. Towards the end of the last century, W. Thompson Watkin, whose books on Roman Cheshire and Roman Lancashire are still treated with respect by modern archaeologists, argued most convincingly that there was nothing Roman about the city walls at all. Others took his arguments further and said they were not even medieval but put up during the Civil War. It is pleasant to be able to record that here the experts were wrong and the traditionalists right. Successive excavations right up to recent times have revealed the outline of the Roman camp and confirmed that its northern and eastern walls lie under the present ones. Documentary evidence and the type of walling make it plain that the big extension on the southern and western sides was made during the twelfth and thirteenth centuries when there was ever-present danger of Welsh attacks. Nor do the plentiful Civil War records give even a suggestion that stone walls were ever raised from foundation level to guard the city for King Charles.

It would be possible to go on. The outside of the cathedral is largely the work of Sir George Gilbert Scott, the great Victorian restorer, and I think that unprejudiced critics, who have looked at the engravings made prior to his work, will admit that visually the cathedral has benefited from what he did. Inside there is not only a great deal of Scott's work and that of an earlier restorer, Hussey, in the fabric, but a wealth of nineteenth- and twentieth-century ironwork, mosaics and painted glass. Most of it is skilful and conscientious: some of it, such as the great west window of 1961 with its glowing colours and tall hieratic figures of Saxon saints, outstanding. Yet what is chiefly remarkable about Chester Cathedral is that it was the church of the great monastery of St Werburgh's and that many of the principal monastic buildings have survived. They were all there at the Dissolution in 1539 and their broad layout had been planned many centuries before.

In effect, within and around the not very large circumference of the walls, the citizens of Chester and its visitors can, if they wish, walk through history. They will see and appreciate it more if they prepare themselves somewhat, for many of the remains of past ages are fragmentary and not very prominent, and their significance not immediately obvious. Despite its '95% Victorian and after', there is no better guide than Pevsner and Hubbard's *Cheshire.* It does not devote 95% – or anything like it – of the 45 pages that describe Chester to the work of the Victorians and those that have come after them. It tells you specifically where you can find the work of all the previous ages. Its treatment is wholly architectural, however, and for knowledge of the people who put up and used the buildings a visit should be made to the Grosvenor Museum in Grosvenor Street. Here there are galleries with exhibits illustrating and explaining life in Chester throughout the ages, and a publications room with books and pamphlets on the same topics for sale.

The finds from Roman Chester have been and continue to be so rich that they and the picture built up from them dominate the Museum. The Newstead Gallery shows by the aid of a diorama, models, drawings and photographs the layout of Deva, the legionary fortress, and the organisation of the xxth Legion that held it during the greater part of its existence. The whereabouts of most of the usual buildings that existed in a large Roman fortress have been discovered by excavation: north of the Via Principalis (the line of Watergate and Eastgate Streets) and in the centre of the fortress, the principium and the praetoria; besides and to the north of these, barrack blocks for the legionaries and workshops; south of the Via Principalis, the baths, the granaries (for the legionaries consumed more bread than meat), and more barrack blocks; to the south-east outside the walls, the amphitheatre. But, to demonstrate that Roman fortress building was not utterly stereotyped and that surprises can occur, during the recent excavations that took place when the Market Hall was rebuilt there emerged just west of the praetoria the partial outlines of a most intriguing building. Rectangular in shape, yet containing within it a large elliptical courtyard, it has no parallel in other Roman fortresses and no one has yet hit upon a satisfactory explanation of its function.

There is a second Roman gallery in the Grosvenor Museum, full of finds made in or near the fortress. Most of these are inscribed stones and mean little to the layman until interpreted. When interpreted (there is a book on them), they reveal fascinating details about the lives of the soldiers: where they came from (all over the vast Empire), whom they prayed to, how long they lived (one to over 80), how some died (one was shipwrecked), how they dressed. In addition there are inscriptions that help to date the stages in the development of the fortress. The interpretations of some of these show the ingenuity as well as the great learning of modern archaeologists. One fragment containing just one whole letter and minute parts of four others has been expanded into an inscription of ten words, which helps to fix the building of the stone fortress within the years 102-18, the later part of the reign of Trajan. A much longer inscription on a piece of lead piping is used to date the earlier fortress, whose turf and timber ramparts lie immediately behind the stone ones of its successor. It was constructed during the 70s of the 1st century A.D., when generals such as Julius Agricola were rapidly pushing Roman dominion northwards.

One of the amazing things about our considerable knowledge of Deva is that almost all of it has come out of the ground. Unlike London, York and Colchester, none of the surviving works of the Roman historians give it a mention. Ptolemy's map and the Antonine road books enable us to fix with certainty that it and the later Chester are on the same site. All other information has been dug up out of the ground or extracted from the walls, like the inscribed tombstones hurriedly pressed into service to strengthen the fortress against unexpected danger. Furthermore, all this has been found, not in an unoccupied countryside, but underneath a living city where thousands of people go about their daily business. Much recent work, undertaken during wholesale redevelopment of the centre of the city, has been done almost literally under the jaws of the mechanical excavators. The evidence, which had lain undisturbed for nearly two thousand years, has now regrettably vanished for ever, but at least knowledge of it has been recorded and added to the patient reconstruction of the city's Roman origins. Chester has been fortunate in having a corporation very proud of the city's past and anxious to increase knowledge of it and, in the curators and staff of the Grosvenor Museum, the initiative and expertise to carry through the excavation work.

Armed with knowledge gained from the Museum, the visitor can make a rapid survey of such Roman remains as are above ground, using the walls as the most convenient route for moving from one site to another. There are patches of Roman walling on the outside of the eastern section of the north wall, and the foundations of a Roman angle tower just north of the Newgate. Near by, in a park, are the bases of pillars and a reconstructed hypocaust, and a little further from the walls half the amphitheatre lies exposed. On the far side of the town, above the Roodee and below the Nuns Road, is a section of a Roman quay that must have stood on a creek that ran up from the Dee. In Hamilton Place, in the side of the new market building, the steps leading down into the strong room of the principium are on view, brought to light in a recent excavation. Above the strong room was the shrine where the standards were kept. The safe keeping of the legion's pay and the surrounding of these military emblems with an atmosphere of religious awe were necessary steps to keep up legionary morale in a distant and by no means wholly subdued country.

How, during the wars of Alfred's successors against the Norsemen in the 10th century, Chester again became an important port and fortress and had a shire constructed around it, has been told in the Introduction. A royal mint was set up in it and, although it had been recreated as a bulwark against them, many Norsemen came to live in it and others to use it for trade, so that it had an accepted position in the Scandinavian seafaring world.

Evidence for these developments comes from manuscripts and coinage. Not even a fragment of a Norse or Saxon building is left above ground in the city. So all the seeker after Saxon Chester can do is to stare across the Dee Bridge towards Edgar Park, once Edgar's Field, and imagine that he sees the eight sub-kings rowing the royal barge in acknowledgment of Edgar's supremacy. Even here it has to be admitted that the rowing incident, while not impossible, is mentioned by no contemporary, and that J. D. Bu'Lock, the historian of Anglo-Saxon Cheshire, thinks the site, although the traditional one, most unlikely. He points out that rowing upstream from the Field to St John's across the weir would have been difficult (even for sub-kings), and that Edgar's palace was probably at Aldford, from which a row downstream to St John's would have been comparatively easy.

Chester was the last important town in England to submit to William the Conqueror, who was so anxious that this submission should not be delayed that he drove his half-mutinous army across the Pennines in the depth of winter to obtain it. The deliberate devastation that they spread over most of the county is plainly shown in Domesday Book, made many years later. In Chester they pulled down half the houses and erected a castle on a mound overlooking the Dee, outside the limit of the Saxon fortifications. Yet the Conqueror's wrath did not prevent Chester from rising soon to yet another period of national importance. His castle passed into the hands of the new Norman Earl of Chester who rebuilt it in stone and much enlarged it. The city became both a bastion and a launching pad in the long struggle with the Welsh, who reacted with fury and, for a time, with considerable success to the Norman attempts to break into the mountainous regions which the Saxons had left severely alone. Chester's walls were also rebuilt in stone and extended west and south to bring under their protection all the dry land within the great curve of the Dee. In those days the Roodee was a stretch of golden sand at low tide, but submerged when the waters were high. Even in the days when Welsh raids went as deep into the county as Nantwich, the defences of Chester were never seriously threatened.

When the climax came at the end of the thirteenth century and Edward I, who was also Earl of Chester, determined to destroy the power of Llywelyn of Gwynedd, who had acquired the title of Prince of Wales,

Chester was for a time almost a second capital. The king, the queen, the great nobles, administrators and courtiers, were frequently in it. Armies and fleets were launched from it along the North Wales coast. In 1283, when Llywelyn had been killed and his brother Dafydd reduced to a hunted fugitive, Edward returned to Chester, heard mass in St Werburgh's and gave the abbey a valuable cloth. It was really a thanksgiving service for the successful conclusion of the war.

There is a certain amount to be seen above ground of these days of Chester's greatness, although no domestic buildings have survived. Fire was a much greater danger to them than Welsh raids, and in 1140, 1180 and 1278 the greater part of the city was burnt down. The twelfth-century remains in the cathedral and in St John's church give some measure of Chester's greatness. St John's has a nave of great round pillars that call to mind Durham or Tewkesbury, but it should be recalled that what stands now is only a shortened relic of what the church once was. The nave was longer and there were transepts and a mighty tower. The church had cathedral status and was actually the seat of the bishop from 1075-95. Presumably he found the attentions of the Welsh too distracting — St John's is outside the walls — and for the remainder of the Middle Ages retired to his alternative seats of Lichfield and Coventry.

There are two sections of twelfth-century work in the great church that is now the cathedral. The rougher and earlier work is the round-arched opening and triforium of six bays in the east wall of the north transept. This would have belonged to the first building phase after the founding of the Benedictine abbey in 1092. The founders were that extraordinary pair of friends, Hugh 'Lupus', first Norman Earl of Chester, and Anselm, abbot of Bec in Normandy; the first violent, lecherous and cunning, the second saintly, scholarly and retiring. Anselm's visit to England and Cheshire was bound up with a plot concocted by Hugh, other great barons and the leading bishops to force the unsuspecting Anselm on the notice of the king, William Rufus, as a suitable archbishop of Canterbury. Rufus was leaving the archbishopric vacant and pocketing its revenues. The scheme succeeded because of a sudden and dangerous illness of the king. But he recovered and the divisions between him and his too saintly archbishop must have made the plotters wonder whether they had been altogether wise.

The beautiful thirteenth-century work in some of the conventual buildings, the rib-vaulting of the chapter house and the stone reading pulpit built into the wall of the monks' refectory (from which passages of the scriptures and the writings of the Holy Fathers were read to the monks during meal times) reflect the prosperous times of this century. The Welsh Wars brought many people and much trade to the city and the abbey, under the rule of wise abbots, was widely respected.

The two lower rooms of the so-called Agricola's tower, the principal survival of the medieval castle, belong to this period also. It was once one of the towers of the inner bailey and the upper of the two rooms was the tiny chapel of St Mary de Castro. The lower room is now the museum of the Cheshire Regiment. But the presence all around the tower of Thomas Harrison's late eighteenth-century Classical Revival buildings is so overwhelming that the atmosphere of the days of the Welsh Wars can better be appreciated by promenading the western section of the city walls.

Most of this is the extension that was made to protect the growing town from Welsh attacks. From it can be seen, looking very close and inviting on clear days, the hills of Wales. Nowadays they have become a Mecca for thousands in search of aesthetic pleasure, rest and recreation. As late as the eighteenth century, Defoe thought them 'a prospect best at a distance'. It is doubtful whether the medieval citizens of Chester and – even more – the inhabitants of the surrounding countryside would have allowed them even that. From them came sudden destruction. Just across the old Dee Bridge is Handbridge. It is Chester's oldest suburb and existed in the twelfth century, yet there are no medieval buildings in it and probably were not even in Tudor times. The Welsh devastated it so frequently that their name for it was *Treboeth* (the *burnt* settlement). Its inhabitants must have had their eyes perpetually on their escape route, the Dee bridge. A timber bridge existed in Norman times and the first stone replacement came in 1280. The citizens, however, could look with greater comfort at the protective curve of the Dee and their ring of battlemented walls with guard towers at intervals. It is no wonder there was a special tax, the murage, for the upkeep of the walls and special officers, the muragers, to see to its collection.

With the next two centuries there was diminution of Chester's importance and prosperity. The city suffered from the ravages of the Black Death and from the increasing lawlessness of the times. There were brawls between citizens and the servants of the monks and between citizens and royal officials. Retainers of quarrelling local lords fought it out in the streets. The abbots of St Werburgh's were men of weak character and poor reputation. The subjugation of North Wales removed the strategic value of Chester and there was increasing worry about the silting up of the river Dee. Nevertheless, there was continued vitality in the city, and work of great distinction, literary as well as architectural, came out of St Werburgh's. One of its monks, Ranulf Higden, was the outstanding chronicler of his day and his *Polychronicon,* a history of the world from the Creation to his own times, was popular enough for an English translation to be brought out shortly after his death. There is a manuscript copy on display in the chapter house. The famous cycle of Mystery Plays, covering the Christian portrayal of the history of the world from the Creation to the Last Judgement and played by the guilds of the city at Whitsuntide, was also written inside the monastery. It has been attributed to particular monks, including Higden, but it is probable that it was the work of many hands, amended and developed over a considerable period. It was in this period also that the wonderful choir stalls were carved, the recognised pious subjects such as the Tree of Jesse and the Coronation of the Virgin openly displayed on the bench ends, the medieval sub-world of fabulous beasts, legendary heroes and everyday low life half hidden under the misericords.

Chester had no intention of tamely surrendering its position as the principal town and port of north-west England, and in Tudor times circumstances gave her an opportunity of recovering something of her importance. The attempts of the monarchs to bring Ireland under closer control and the religious differences brought about by the Reformation resulted in a series of Irish risings. An increasing number of royal officials, heavier consignments of troops and government-encouraged Protestant colonists all needed to be transported to Ireland. There was still no town comparable to Chester as a port of transit. It was convenient for Dublin, large enough for accommodation, with good communication lines to the south and east. Liverpool still lacked these, was too small and remote, and not without its own difficulties regarding its harbourage and seaways. Chester corporation, therefore, were able to get government backing for the series of outports which were built up along the estuary of the Dee and could take her seagoing vessels. (Something is said about these in the chapter on the Wirral.) By such means she was able to keep her own trade going: a brisk export of calfskins, imports of French and Spanish wines and Spanish iron, the providing of supplies for the troops in Ireland. So she remained up to the time of the Civil Wars a busy and reasonably prosperous town.

It is in this period from 1485 to 1642 that the Rows appear unmistakably in the form in which we know them today and are recognised as a speciality of Chester. The form is that of a double row of shops, the lower at just below street level and bearing upon it a gallery, providing access to the upper shops which are recessed. There is yet another storey above these shops which oversails the gallery and is supported on it by wooden pillars. The origins of the structures obviously go back a long time before the Tudor period, and there is great controversy as to their nature. It is not likely to be resolved because no domestic buildings survive from these earlier times, and although the term *row* appears in the town records from the fourteenth century on it could mean no more than a line of houses. The oldest buildings now standing in the Rows all date from Tudor and Stuart times. The best and least altered, such as the Leche House and Bishop Lloyd's House, are in Watergate Street. It is in this period also that the town records make it plain that they are referring to an unusual type of building, and that the topographers begin to take note. John Leland paralleled Chester's Rows with some streets in Bridgnorth which seem to have vanished since without trace, but by Elizabethan times William Smith, the Cheshire-born cartographer, was proudly declaring, 'which maner of building I have not hard of in any place of Christendome'. All commentators commended them for 'keeping a man dry in foul weather'. But the criticism appeared early in the seventeenth century that they made the streets dark, and this began to outweigh all other considerations when the Age of Enlightenment arrived. Celia Fiennes, that apostle of the modern and progressive, was positive that they detracted from the beauty of the streets, while Defoe went further:

'They take away all the view of the houses from the streets . . . besides they make the shops themselves dark and the way in them is dark, dirty and uneven.'

Presumably this is the starting point for that most flippant and scandalous of all theories concerning the origin of the Rows: that they were not improvised to go on top of massive Roman remains, borrowed from Scandinavia or thought up after the fire of 1278 to give protection from sudden incursions by the Welsh, but deliberately constructed to ensure that Chester shopkeepers would never have to display their wares in plain daylight.

It was perhaps fortunate that Antiquarianism came in with the Enlightenment. By 1773 Thomas Pennant was speaking of 'these streets without parallel' and postulating a Roman origin. This spirit and the Chester shopkeepers' dislike of being disturbed probably saved them from the fate of the medieval castle and town gates, swept away in Thomas Harrison's great rebuilding programme of 1780-1810.

It has been said by one of those who hold that Chester's decline from the fourteenth century on was steep and unchecked, that 'The agony of the Civil War siege, the last spasm of importance, happened almost by accident.' Chester citizens, proud of their forbears' devotion to the cause of monarchy, are not likely to accept such a verdict, and it is difficult to justify from contemporary evidence. This indicates that a siege of Chester was inevitable once King Charles's cause began to lose ground in the north and he tried to counter this by making a truce with the Irish Catholic rebels and bringing over units of his army in Ireland which had been fighting them. The siege was protracted for many reasons. Chester was protected by the river and extensive marshes, and guarded by old medieval walls and new earth ramparts and ditches covering the suburbs. The citizens were genuinely loyal to King Charles, and scared of the vengeance which the besieging Roundhead general, Sir William Brereton, a Cheshire squire with a long record of lawsuits and altercations with the city, might exact. They raised a defence force of nearly 1,000, a large Home Guard for a comparatively small city. Extra troops for the garrison were available from North Wales and from the army in Ireland. Parliament could spare none of its main armies and Brereton's besieging force had to be built up bit by bit by bringing in local forces from all over the north-west and the Midlands. His headaches in provisioning, quartering and paying this motley army and preventing the units from different counties from flying at each others' throats, occupy a far greater space in his correspondence than does fighting against the enemy.

Brereton himself said, 'They will never lose their whole interest at once in all these north-west parts of the kingdom', and whenever it looked as if Chester might fall, royalist headquarters set forces in motion for its relief. So the siege went on for over a year. The original blockade was lifted by King Charles himself at the head of the main royalist army. After its defeat at Naseby, the suburbs were stormed, but Charles's fleeting reappearance with a much smaller force and an all-out resistance in which civilians, including women, assisted the soldiers, prevented attempts to break into the city itself. Brereton then assembled a large artillery train and began to batter the town day and night. Scarcely a house in the Rows was left undamaged, several were flattened completely and the inhabitants took refuge in the medieval crypts and cellars for days on end, like Londoners in the tubes during the Blitz. But the soldiers were largely unharmed and the terror only seemed to stiffen resistance. So a much tighter blockade was set up. Finally, the absence of any royalist army able to effect relief and the threat of starvation brought surrender.

The damage done to the city, by Civil War standards, was enormous. The papers of Randle Holmes, one of the city's aldermen, gives a great list of buildings destroyed and adds that the cost to the city of the expenses of the defence and the loss of their stocks, plate and rents must have been £200,000 at least. Many of the buildings were not destroyed by enemy action but pulled down by the defenders, usually to aid in the defence. A relic connected with the siege is the Phoenix Tower in the north-east angle of the walls. It has been renamed King Charles's tower because he stood there to watch the battle which occurred halfway through the siege. The main engagement was on Rowton Moor south-east of the city between forces arriving for the relief of both sides, but there was also fire interchanged between the garrison behind the old walls and the besiegers who were by this time established in the eastern suburbs. In the summer months the tower houses a small but interesting collection of Civil War relics. There are also, just outside the Newgate, the reconstructed fragments of the old High Cross which was broken down by Brereton's soldiers when they entered the city after the surrender. It seems to have been their sole action of this kind, however. Brereton himself, although a Puritan, was no lover of destruction and, as we know from his travel journals, had a taste for architecture. Much of the glass in the cathedral and other churches seems to have survived the Civil War

4 *The medieval bridge at Chester with, in the foreground, the remains of the old causeway that supplied power to the mills, and in the background New County Hall and St Mary's church.*

and fallen victim to the fury of the ultra-Protestant city mob during the visit of Monmouth in 1682.

It probably took Chester 50 years or more to recover fully from the effects of the Civil War; added to which the continued silting of the Dee was extinguishing her outports one by one. To deal with this the citizens showed continuing vitality and aided by surrounding Cheshire and Flintshire squires got the Dee canalised in the 1730s. The results of this can be seen by going through the Watergate and along New Crane Street and Sealand Road. On the right the Dee Basin, the new dock that was made, has now been filled in, but on the left the windings of the Dee end abruptly with a canalised stretch which takes the waters away south-westwards towards the Flintshire side of the estuary. It was a brave effort and enabled Chester just to stagger through as a port for ocean-going vessels into the age of steam and iron.

When the growing size of vessels and railway competition finally brought the port to an end, what had probably been true all through Chester's long history was made plain. Her importance did not depend on her port. It is highly unlikely that even in the days of the Roman fortress and the Saxon and medieval city, their remote and not very accessible harbour could have been on a level with the ports of the south and east. Perhaps more symptomatic of Chester's continuing *raison d'être* than Harrison's pillared and pedimented 'Castle' or Douglas and Lockwood's revivalist black and white houses, are Grosvenor Street, the lovely arch of the Grosvenor Bridge (also designed by Harrison) and Chester General Station. Chester from Roman times on was the hub of the communication routes between North Wales and the rest of Britain. When the coaching age got under way, a new road and an additional bridge had to be made out of Chester. With the railway age scarcely begun, lines were running in from Crewe, Birkenhead and Shrewsbury and a much greater one under construction to Holyhead to make a new link with Ireland. Hence Chester General, the largest and most impressive Victorian building in Chester.

The motor age has reinforced this truth, not wholly to the comfort of Chester's citizens or the peace of mind of her administrators. H. V. Morton, who got to Chester just before it came in, was able to speak of 'this silent city where old houses dream across old streets'. There is not much silence nor dreaming, even at night time, in Chester now. Traffic

Gawsworth church tower, with Lord Mohun's school, now the rectory, in front.

roars through constantly, houses are pulled down to make way for car parks which fill to overflowing as soon as they are opened. An inner ring road on the west and an incredibly complicated system of re-routing on the eastern approaches have prevented utter strangulation, but only just. The Rows have once again proved their worth by saving the lives and sanity of shoppers until shopping precincts could be built and pedestrian areas laid down.

It is not just a question of through traffic. Chester is a busy centre, crowded by shoppers from a wide surrounding area in almost any season, by tourists in the summer, by those coming in for the Races, for the Regattas, for festivals and other cultural activities and in order to visit the highly successful post-Second World War Zoo at Upton Park. Local government changes at the end of the nineteenth century made it the centre for an ever-expanding county administration; recent changes have added to this the administration of the south-west district of the new county. It has been labelled 'a tired old city' by one of the believers in the myth of its progressive decline since the fourteenth century. A *tiring* old — and new — city, perhaps, but hardly *tired*.

TWO

The Wirral

'Wirral, a piece of land between the seas behind Chester.'

This was the bald description sent by Sir William Brereton to a Roundhead colleague in the south to let him know where he was campaigning. Wirral was an obscure offshoot of a region still remote enough to a dweller in the south-east. To those nearer at hand both the climate and the inhabitants had a reputation for wildness. In the fourteenth century the anonymous author of *Sir Gawayne and the Green Knight* spoke of:

> 'The wilderness of Wirral: few lived there
> Who loved with a good heart either God or man.'

In the late nineteenth century, James Stonehouse, a Liverpool nonagenarian, recalling the days of his youth, spoke of Wallasey people as 'very fiends'. He was referring to their notorious wrecking activities, which thrived on the booming trade of Liverpool, the wild gales and swift currents which made their section of coastline dangerous to shipping, and the marshes and frequent flooding which often islanded their hideouts.

Yet there were, and still are, compensating features in the climate and soil of the Wirral. The sunshine is far more frequent, the rainfall much less than in eastern Cheshire and many other parts of England. The heavy boulder clay is tempered by alluvium and blown sand, and all over the peninsula the sandstone rock breaks through to the surface. Thus there were 'dry points' for early settlement and soil suitable for primitive cultivation. If the mouth of the Mersey was narrow and hard to find for sailors without charts or compasses, the mouth of the Dee was wide open and right alongside its entrance was the Hyle or Hoyle Lake, a natural anchorage formed by shore, islands and sand banks.

The Hoyle Lake did not finally disappear until the eighteenth century. Finds made off Dove Point in the nineteenth century, when erosion laid bare the 'sunken forest', suggest that it had been in existence for thousands of years and was the meeting place of traffic across the Irish Sea. The northern coast of Wirral seems to have had a thriving settlement at Meols when most of the rest of the region that was to become Cheshire was either inhabited thinly or not at all.

The Norsemen, coming over usually after a spell in Ireland, settled all over the peninsula. Fragments of their wheel-headed crosses and grave slabs can be seen in the Grosvenor Museum and at Neston and West Kirby churches. The names of their villages lie thick on the face of the land: Pensby, Greasby, Kirby, Irby, Raby, Meols, Tranmere, Thingwall. At the time of Domesday Book the Wirral was, together with the area south of Chester, the most thickly populated part of an admittedly not very populous county. The Survey shows it studded with manorial villages and containing the largest manor in the county, Eastham.

During the Middle Ages other areas of the county caught up with and sometimes surpassed the Wirral. Its afforestation from Norman times until 1376 certainly did not help agricultural development. For, although it did not necessarily mean that the ground was covered with trees, the needs of the farmer were put a long way behind the preservation of game. Upper Deeside remained important, however, and tolerably populous and prosperous. In the time of the Welsh Wars, Shotwick Castle guarded fords which were the best route into North Wales, while the arm of Burton Head sheltered an anchorage where men and supplies could be embarked.

By the time of the Tudors and Stuarts, although the fords of the upper Dee were still much in use, silting had made Shotwick and Burton impracticable for seagoing vessels and outports had to be developed further down the river. For, as mentioned in the previous chapter, Chester was incomparably the best base from which to despatch the increasing number of troops and supplies needed to control Ireland. The brief survey of the Wirral made by John Leland in the reign of Henry VIII shows how much Deeside overshadowed in importance the rest of the peninsula. He details all the villages and halls and all the 'rodes' where ships could lie at anchor from Chester to the mouth of the Dee. From then on he mentions only Wallasey, 'where men use much to salten hering', and the dissolved priory of Birkenhead. Of the interior he says nothing at all.

The eighteenth century saw the Wirral relapse into obscurity. The canalisation of the upper estuary of the Dee in 1737 and further silting at its mouth spelt the doom of Chester's outports. The new lines of communication, the river navigations and canals which were linking Liverpool to the Lancashire and Cheshire hinterland, missed the Wirral altogether. At the beginning of the nineteenth century its total population was just under 12,000, as against 212,000 for the rest of the county, and the only township in it with a population over 1,000 was Neston-cum-Parkgate. John Aikin's famous *Description of the Country from Thirty to Forty Miles around Manchester* did not include an account of the Wirral, although it was within his prescribed limit. Having no canals and showing little or no industrial or agricultural development, the region held no interest for him.

In 1815 the first steam ferry ran across the Mersey. By the 1830s there were enough ferries for wealthy Liverpool businessmen to commute daily to Birkenhead, where previously there had only been a hamlet and a ruined priory. By 1851 its population had risen from just over 100 to 24,000. Docks and industry had come, although much opposed by those in charge of Liverpool's destiny. Commuting from Liverpool remained, however, the dominant theme of the development of the Wirral. From 1866 to 1888 Birkenhead was linked to its northern and western coasts by a network of railway lines. In 1888 the railway tunnel under the Mersey was opened. No longer need Liverpool commuters sit, like Nathaniel Hawthorne, in their villas in Rock Park and gaze out on the Mersey's 'mudpuddly hue' and banks of 'glistening mud'. They could go further afield to Great Neston, Heswall, West Kirby and Hoylake and view the open sea and the panorama of the Welsh mountains. Pevsner and Hubbard have proclaimed the acme of delectable suburbia to be in the tree-lined roads that rise up the slopes of Caldy and Grange Hills. 'By reason of its prosperous commuter country Cheshire is something of a Surrey of the north, but Surrey has nothing to compare with this.'

In the twentieth century the coming of the private car and the motor bus have widened the range of the commuting classes from a clique of wealthy merchants to almost the whole community. In recent years the housing estates of Birkenhead have pushed right across the middle of the peninsula. When in 1974 two-thirds of the Wirral was included in the metropolitan area of Merseyside centred on Liverpool, administration was simply brought into line with what had been day to day reality for many decades. Probably in no other part of Britain has the character of a region been so completely changed in the last 150 years.

Nowadays, the traveller going out of the Watergate towards the Wirral drives first over the dead-flat expanse of Sealand, reclaimed from the bed of the river and officially in North Wales. The line of the old Cheshire shore can be seen away to the right as a series of low bluffs running as far as Burton Point. Although the New Cut was opened in 1737, it was not until 1916 that the last great 'cop' or embankment was finally secured, so that, even with the highest tide and the strongest wind, the waters would lap no more round the graveyard at Shotwick church. Shotwick castle, where Edward I and his queen once stayed, is a series of bumps in a field. There is no trace of 'the Kyng's Highway ner Chester to lede the hoost of our Sovreyn lord the Kyng in tyme of warre unto Shotwyk Ford', nor of the line of the ford to which it led. In any case we know that this shifted constantly. The Roundhead soldiers, when they abandoned the siege of Hawarden castle in 1645, crossed to Puddington. In 1698 Celia Fiennes reached the Cheshire shore at Burton. She was told of whole carriages swallowed up in new-made hollows in the sands, when the travellers had trusted to knowledge of the route that was not up to date.

Of buildings contemporary with the area's long-forgotten maritime and military past there is only Shotwick church with its Norman south doorway and late medieval fabric. Of the last days of the old estuary and its fords there is more. Shotwick Hall is a delightful brick building of 1662 with a gabled porch and large gabled wings. Its squires, the Hockenhulls, managed to keep themselves well out of sight in the troubles of this century. Their neighbours, the Masseys of Puddington, descended from a junior branch of the Norman house of Dunham Massey, were less fortunate. They were heavily fined as delinquents after the Civil War, although their crime seems to have been more that they were Papists than active supporters of King Charles. During the anti-Catholic scare of Charles II's reign, their chaplain was dragged from the priest's hole in their hall, tried at Chester and executed. The last of the line died in Chester gaol in 1716, suspected of Jacobitism. Tradition has it that he was out in the '15, fled for home from the disastrous fight at Preston, and his horse, after swimming the Mersey, dropped dead in the courtyard of the Hall. The courtyard, its surrounding buildings timber-framed and dating from Tudor times, is still there. Both Shotwick and Puddington Halls are now farmhouses.

Burton has a church rebuilt almost entirely in 1721, and little altered by the Victorians, a measure of the village's unimportance in their day. In the wide village street are many old cottages built on outcrops of sandstone rock, but Burton is chiefly noted for educational landmarks. On the road to Ness is the school, founded in 1724 by Thomas Wilson, bishop of Sodor and Man, who was born in the village. An austere and dedicated man, he spent his life trying to provide schools for the education of all. Although he was too modest to allow his name to be inscribed on a commemorative stone, the school was always known as Bishop Wilson's school and was run on the lines he laid down until 1881, when it became part of the state system. The buildings were then modified and enlarged, and have only just been abandoned for a new school on the south side of the village. By this time fresh educational distinction had been bestowed on Burton. Its Manor, which had been rebuilt in classical style in 1906 for one of Gladstone's sons, had become Cheshire's residential college for Adult Education.

Below Burton Point there are no more 'cops' nor official land reclamation. The river comes no more to Ness and Neston, however, and only on the highest tides to Parkgate. Here, up to the Second World War, children played on the sands and fishing boats anchored off the front. Then the saltings took over. First a layer of mud; then tufts of glasswort; then coarse grass, sedges and rushes. The river, over on the Flintshire side, is barely visible now. Below Heswall, however, the shore is still a shore, and what is exposed at low water is sand rather than mud. The whole area is a kind of demi-seaside suburbia, interspersed with dwindling patches of farming land.

Here from the sixteenth to the eighteenth centuries were the outports, developed to keep the seaway to Chester open. The building of the New

Haven was begun in the reign of Henry VIII with backing from the Privy Council and, although we know a too-ambitious scheme had to be curtailed, we presume the result was the 'New Key', marked on the maps of Saxton and Speed and described by Webb. All site it near to Great Neston, which Webb said was a place many people were better acquainted with than they desired to be, through having to wait there for a wind for Ireland. Later in the seventeenth century, the main embarkation point shifted downstream to Parkgate, and later still to Dawpool, earlier known as Red Bank.

Many people of note used these embarkation points. There were the Lord Deputies of Ireland, including the most famous of them, Strafford. There was William of Orange, who spent the night before he sailed at Gayton Hall, which still stands although refronted. There were Handel, Wesley and Dean Swift. Visible remains are few and doubtful. The quayside of substantial sandstone blocks, lying a mile south-west of Neston church on the old shore line, must presumably be the New Key of Saxton, Speed and Webb. (It has been marked *Old Quay* on maps for the past 100 years, but all New Keys must, if they survive, in time become Old Quays). But the jetty half a mile up river is a mystery. It seems probable that it was constructed later, not as an outport, but to embark coals for Ireland. For hereabouts was the Wirral's only relic of the first Industrial Revolution.

Sir John Stanley of Hooton, who succeeded by marriage to the estates of the Masseys of Puddington, opened a colliery near Ness in the late eighteenth century. By the time it closed in the nineteenth century, there was a second colliery further down river. Although started by the Cottinghams, who were the landlords, it was bought by some Lancashire merchants who called themselves The Neston Colliery Company. Increasingly they used the new railway line rather than the jetty. The workings of both collieries went deep under the bed of the Dee, the seams were thin and the coal of poor quality. Yet such was the demand for coal prior to 1914 and such the conservative and localised nature of the British coal industry, that the Neston Colliery, under the new name of The Wirral Colliery, lasted until just after the disastrous coal strike of 1926. Its slag heaps still lie alongside the shore, there are photographs of it and its last shift in the Harp Inn, and a handful of men in the area once worked in its mines as youngsters.

Parkgate's quay is presumably embedded in the present promenade. Its last days as a packet station overlapped with its brief spell as a fashionable watering place. Sea bathing was regarded at first as a cure for ailments rather than a pleasure; nevertheless a visitor to Parkgate in 1813 was shocked by 'the groups of women . . . jumping, shouting, laughing and screaming', and not thinking it 'necessary to hide themselves under the awnings of bathing machines'.

The 'quality' vanished when the railways brought trippers, but its sands and its inshore fishing boats made Parkgate popular, the latter providing the shrimps for the famous teas. Visitors still come, although rarely with children, and there are still shrimp teas, although the shrimps are imported. Little remains of Parkgate's eighteenth-century elegance, although many of the buildings are still there, hidden behind late nineteenth- and twentieth-century façades.

A little line of sandstone blocks on the shore between Caldy and Thurstaston are probably the remains of the Dawpool quay. Some have thought them the abandoned beginning of Telford's Wirral canal scheme of the 1820s. This, which was initiated by William Laird, was for docks in Wallasey Pool and a ship canal across North Wirral. Its exit into the Dee, however, was not to be at Dawpool, but at West Kirby into a tidal basin formed by embankments running out to Hilbre Island. But there was a parallel scheme set on foot by Manchester businessmen for a ship canal running through North Cheshire to Ellesmere Port, which was then to cross the Wirral to a dock at Dawpool. In any case, the swift intervention of Liverpool interests crushed both schemes long before they got to the building stage.

When the Manchester Ship Canal was eventually built, it came out into the Mersey and not the Dee. But there have been, and still are, schemes to utilise the waters of the Dee once more: to dredge its channels so that ocean-going vessels can use it again, to build a hydro-electricity plant on it, to convert it into a freshwater reservoir to meet the ever-increasing demands of nearby conurbations. Only the last, the Dee Barrage scheme, involving an embankment across the Dee estuary which would also serve to drain off the heavy North Wales traffic from the Queensferry route, remains under serious consideration at the moment.

Cheshire's ten miles of genuine sea coast between the mouths of the Dee and the Mersey has been thoroughly tamed and urbanised. An embankment with promenade runs almost the whole way along it and, until the recent local government changes, control was shared by the county borough of Wallasey and the urban district of Hoylake. There are not houses all the way, but where there are not the ground is taken up by such very civilised institutions as the Royal Liverpool Golf Club at Hoylake.

At the beginning of the eighteenth century this sea coast presented a very different appearance. Hoylake was still only the name for a piece of the sea. There were two houses and a royal storehouse at the point where King William embarked for the Boyne campaign in 1690. Round the Red Rocks Point was the little fishing village of West Kirby, whose ten taverns could only be justified to the magistrates on the grounds of supplying the needs of soldiers waiting for embarkation. Hilbre, a mile offshore, is now the delight of the bird watcher, the botanist, the geologist and the sun bather, but the normal comment on it then was 'a barren little island', or 'nothing could be more wild and dreary'.

In the centre of the coastline was the region known as the 'Leasowes'. The inhabitants of its farms and tiny hamlets numbered only a few hundred, and its most noteworthy features were sand dunes and the old towered residence of the earls of Derby, whose semi-derelict condition had given it the name of Mockbeggar Hall. The 'Leasowes' was only well populated when armies encamped there waiting for a wind to take them from the Hoyle Lake to Ireland. The last large army to come was King William's in 1689. Its commander was an ex-marshal of France and among his troops were French Huguenots, Dutch, Germans, Danes, Swedes and even Finns. What the few natives thought of this polyglot horde and what they thought of northern Wirral is unrecorded.

The fantastic growth of Liverpool in the eighteenth century did not spill over into the Wirral, whose population rose little. As far as northern Wirral was concerned, however, the rise of Liverpool undoubtedly added interest, variety and sometimes profit to the lives of its inhabitants, although in ways that were not always creditable. Liverpool's main seaway, until Captain (afterwards Admiral) Denham surveyed the Crosby Channel running north along the Lancashire coast in the 1830s, was through the Rock and Horse Channels past the Wirral shore. The channels were tricky and tended to alter, and the chances of being driven ashore in a westerly gale were very great. A link with these times can be seen in the lighthouses at Hoylake, Leasowe, Bidston Hill, and at the Perch Rock at the mouth of the Mersey. All have been rebuilt since the eighteenth century; indeed the Perch Rock derived its name from the 'perch' or great pole with a beacon and a vane on it, which was the crude predecessor of the later lighthouse. This is the only one of the Wirral lighthouses to remain operational and that only by remote control. Their day was over by 1914, when the channels were less and less used and could be more accurately indicated by lightships and lighted buoys.

They had never been able to prevent wild weather and many wrecks. Although Wirral men never got quite the horrific reputation of Cornishmen for deliberately luring distressed ships to their doom, stories of their rapacity and lack of piety or charity have passed into folk myth. (In extenuation it should be remembered that they were a very poor community, and all this wealth flowing past their doors which they could never hope to share legitimately was a great temptation.) 'Good Lord, send us a wreck before morning' was alleged to have been the favourite form of prayer in Wallasey, and their parson, when news of a wreck came in during sermon time, was rumoured to have called to his churchwardens to lock the doors until he got down from the pulpit and changed his gown. 'Then we all start fair.'

There has only recently been removed from the front at Egremont the much-altered building that was once known as Mother Redcap's Tavern. Its cellars, concealed passageways and viewpoints covering the mouth of the river and the surrounding countryside made it the favourite haunt, not only of wreckers, but of smugglers and the crews of privateers bent on keeping their persons and their prize money out of the hands of the press gang. The adoption of a new channel by Liverpool shipping, the opening up of communications in the Wirral itself and the arrival of the modern police brought these activities to a halt in mid-nineteenth century.

The ultimate destiny of northern Wirral appeared very slowly. As far back as the seventeenth century Wallasey was known for its race course, although, in actual fact, this began half-a-mile west of the village and continued almost to Mockbeggar Hall. It attracted national attention in 1682, when the Duke of Monmouth who visited it during his tour of Cheshire, won 'the 12 stone plate'. Anxious agents reported back to the government on his conduct at the meeting, the warmth of his reception and the local gentry to whom he paid most attention. In the early eighteenth century an annual race run there attracted considerable prize money from wealthy Cheshire gentry, and the Wallasey stakes at Newmarket and even the Derby are said to be offshoots of it.

In the late eighteenth century Sir John Stanley built a hotel at the fishing hamlet of Hoylake, and Lewis Boode, a wealthy West Indian planter, took over Mockbeggar Hall. Boode and his military son-in-law, Sir Edward Cust, turned it into Leasowe 'Castle', with 'Gothick' alterations and additions. It survives as a Railwaymen's Convalescent Home. They and Sir John were probably the first to consider that residence on the Wirral sea coast might be desirable because of its scenery and romantic associations. (Cust, on little evidence, thought Leasowe the scene of Canute's encounter with the tide and his rebuke to his courtiers, and there is a legend of a mermaid connected with the spot.) But it was not until the coming of the steam ferry boats that these ideas could be exploited further. Then James Atherton and John Agnew, Liverpool merchants, bought uninhabited land at the river mouth and further upstream and founded New Brighton and Egremont. The second name is said to have been taken from Agnew's home village in Cumberland.

Atherton and Agnew intended to set up fashionable seaside resorts. Subsequent developments — the growth of industry around Birkenhead, the opening up of the further side of the Wirral by the railways, the inundation of the Mersey side by day trippers brought over on the ferries — frustrated these intentions. Egremont became a residential suburb of the new town of Wallasey, New Brighton looked like becoming New Blackpool. It acquired a tower larger than Blackpool's, an amusement palace, a floral pavilion and winter gardens. On a hastily erected promenade the 'Ham and Egg Parade' grew up, a ramshackle collection of side-shows, cheap lodgings and eating houses. The depression after the First World War and the wishes of the middle-class residents of the rest of Wallasey halted these developments, however. The great tower came down in 1921; the Wallasey town council had bought up and pulled down the Ham and Egg Parade some time before, substituting a wide promenade and boating lake. New Brighton became a more decorous, if less zestful, resort.

Wallasey itself became the third largest town in the old Cheshire, with a population of over 100,000 and county borough status. Its growth was signalised by the building of a dignified town hall in 1914 on a dominant site overlooking the Mersey. Yet the town hall, with nothing else suggesting a centre about it and over a mile from the site of the old village of Wallasey, only emphasises that modern Wallasey is hardly a town at all. It began as one village with a scattering of colonies of newly erected 'villas'. It has become a vast riverside suburb, whose centre is not even in neighbouring Birkenhead but across the river in Liverpool.

'It is said that *they* [the disciples of progress] have great faith in the future of Birkenhead', wrote Disraeli in 1857 in his novel *Tancred,* at the end of a passage on urban splendour which brought in Babylon, Damascus, Rome, Paris and London! The contemporary press cried:

'The village of but yesterday is raised
To be a populous city, a rich mart –'
and
'Another glory on the Mersey's side.'

It is hardly surprising that Birkenhead has failed to live up to these tremendous trumpetings. Although there was plenty of initiative and vision among its founding fathers their difficulties were great. Their visions were frequently contradictory. F. R. Price, lord of the manor of Birkenhead and original owner of most of the land round about, envisaged the development of a seaside resort serving Liverpool. William Laird, the great pioneer of iron shipbuilding, wanted an industrial port, with docks, shipyards and factories, which necessitated working-class housing. The atmosphere of a boom town did not favour consistent planning. The Lairds and their rivals, the Jackson brothers, were both guilty of reselling land which they had bought because of the profits its enhanced price produced, when they should have held on to it to further their schemes for the development of the town. A feud sprang up between the Lairds and the Jacksons and their supporters, arising partly from their conflicting business interests, partly from their differing national politics and partly from pure personal rivalry. Finally, and worst of all, in the background stood the corporation of Liverpool, always suspicious of, and usually openly hostile to, the creation of 'Another glory on the Mersey's side'.

Telford's original scheme of 1825 for extensive docks in Wallasey Pool, with a canal for ocean-going vessels crossing the Wirral to West

Kirby, although sponsored by Laird, was wrecked by Liverpool corporation buying up land essential to the scheme, some of it owned by Laird himself. Laird persevered with his shipbuilding on Wallasey Pool, however, and his son, John, was able to acquire a site on Merseyside itself for greatly enlarged ship-building yards. There under the name of Cammell, Laird and Co. the firm still is.

By this time the population of Birkenhead had increased enormously, there were considerable business interests in the town and a Board of Improvement Commissioners had been formed to run the town's affairs. Backed by the railways and business interests in Manchester, they were able to get a second docks scheme passed by Parliament. Liverpool, under heavy pressure because the shipping crowding into the Mersey was too great for its existing dock facilities and there were long delays before the ships could berth and discharge, relented to the extent of reselling some of its land on the Wirral side. Hence the launching of the scheme and the opening of the first dock in 1847 to the accompaniment of the golden prophecies quoted above. But the scheme was too ambitious, the difficulties encountered in carrying it out great and the engineer chosen, J. M. Rendel, although he had won great triumphs in the past, unable to cope with them. After only two small docks had been completed, the Egerton and the Morpeth, the money ran out and Liverpool corporation bought up the enterprise. Pressure from Laird, Manchester business interests and the railways continued, and, anxious to get Parliamentary consent for an extension of their own docks, Liverpool agreed to the formation of the Mersey Docks and Harbour Board, a public trust controlling the docks on both sides of the Mersey. Under its control a much modified version of the original scheme for Birkenhead's docks was completed in 1863. As we shall see in the next chapter, Manchester business interests were by no means wholly satisfied and, in the trade depression of the 1880s, returned to the abandoned scheme of their own ship canal.

Meantime the planning for Birkenhead town itself had gone awry. F. R. Price encouraged the setting up of hotels and villas on the original headland where the ruined priory stood. William Laird brought in an Edinburgh architect, J. G. Graham, who produced an ambitious gridiron plan of streets and squares, consisting entirely of substantial stone-faced buildings. With the failure of the original docks scheme, wealthy citizens did not flock to Birkenhead as quickly as the promoters had hoped. Hamilton Square, the centre of Graham's scheme, took from 1825 to 1846 to complete, and many of the other streets, although their lines were laid out, were never built. Meantime the shifting of Laird's shipbuilding yards to the riverside ended all future for the hotels and villas on the headland and necessitated working-class housing close at hand. This was run up haphazard, not only bearing no relation to the original plan but sometimes obviously at odds with the effect it was supposed to create. The meanderings of Borough Road are a glaring example. The driving through of railway lines, not allowed for in the original plan, increased the confusion.

It should not be thought, however, that nothing was accomplished in the building of Birkenhead, and that there is therefore nothing worth looking at. The very considerable achievements tend to be overlooked because so much more was promised. Hamilton Square, built in a kind of dour North-British classical style with grey-white sandstone blocks from the nearby Storeton quarries, has immense dignity. Birkenhead Park, the first park ever to be provided at public expense, is a landmark in the history of local government and the provision of public amenities. It is also a very beautiful park, for the commissioners, driven on by William Jackson's initiative and determination, employed Joseph Paxton to lay it out, and Paxton used, for the first time for the delight of the general public, landscaping techniques which had hitherto only been applied to the surroundings of stately homes. Birkenhead Borough Council, the successor to the Commissioners, remained very park-conscious. At various times it acquired Thurstaston Common, Bidston Hill and Arrow Park, as open spaces for the public to enjoy and 'lungs' for its expanding population.

Birkenhead led the way, too, in the provision of leafy and spacious suburbs. Quite a number of terraces and villas of the 1840s and 1850s, classical and gothic in design, remain in Clifton Park and Claughton. Rock Park, outside the boundaries of the town when it was begun in 1836, was really an extension of F. R. Price's scheme for a watering place on Birkenhead headland. It was far enough south to escape absorption in the dockland that sprang up there in the 1850s, and Nathaniel Hawthorne, who resided in it at the time, commented on its hushed and secluded atmosphere. Nevertheless it was next door to dockland and, although its buildings survive (precariously because of bypass schemes), the wealthy inhabitants have long since moved further afield.

Another experiment in which Birkenhead took the lead has left no visual trace. In 1860 it was the first town in Europe to allow G. F. Train, an ebullient American promoter, to lay down tram lines. They ran from the ferry to Birkenhead Park and he was to take them up again at his own expense if they proved unsuccessful. In fact, they inaugurated for the whole of Europe an era in which the daily functioning of large towns depended on the tram routes which brought workers in from the suburbs.

All Merseysiders with a sense of the past shake their heads sadly over the state of shipping on the river now. There are freighters passing through to the Manchester Ship Canal. There are large tankers making their way to the Queen Elizabeth Dock at Eastham, and larger tankers turning in to the deep water terminals at Tranmere, the oil from all going by pipe lines to the refineries at Stanlow. It seems likely that there will be even larger tankers not coming into the Mersey at all, but turning round off the coast of Anglesey, to which pipe lines will stretch from Stanlow. There are grain ships docking at the Gladstone Docks, Liverpool, and at Bootle, which is really outside the Mersey altogether. No longer is it possible for anyone residing near the river bank to gaze out, as Hawthorne once did, and see a great liner lying in midstream, smoke rising from her gently hours after she anchored, 'as if she were smoking her pipe after her toilsome passage across the Atlantic'. The great liners, themselves a dying breed, come no more to the Mersey. Nor do the smaller ships of all shapes and all nations which used to swarm through the Narrows and lie up in the Sloyne, waiting for docking space. Yet, perhaps, what saddens the historically-minded dwellers on Wirral's Merseyside most of all is the withering away of their ferries, which were almost their only link with the distant past and the main cause of their present existence.

By the fourteenth century the monks of Birkenhead were operating a ferry from the Cheshire side, and there was a royal ferry from Liverpool. After the dissolution of the priory, the ferry was continued by the purchasers of the monastic lands, and between them and the lessees of the royal ferry there was a good deal of squabbling over the stealing of each others' passengers. During all this time there were also ferries to Liverpool operating from Eastham and Seacombe.

6 above The late medieval mill, Nether Alderley. 7 below Siddington church, with genuine timber chancel and brick west front painted to resemble timbering.

In the eighteenth century the number and importance of the ferries increased, all the more because there was no good road from Liverpool, despite the growth both of the port and of coaching. This seems the inescapable conclusion to be drawn from the absence of a main road to Liverpool in Ogilby's route maps, and the actions of Nicholas Blundell as recorded in his diary in 1709. Journeying from Crosby, north of Liverpool, to Whitchurch in Shropshire, he missed the Liverpool ferry and rode on to Runcorn before he could get across the Mersey. Returning, he missed the boat again, this time at Rock Ferry, and went on to Woodside. He never seems to have contemplated taking the all-land route via Warrington. This is all the more surprising when the dangers and discomforts of the crossings are realised. Throughout the eighteenth century passengers were landed at Liverpool in the manner which Defoe describes; 'on the shoulders of some honest Lancashire clown', who shook them worse than 'a hard trotting horse'. The boats were open or half-decked. James Stonehouse, the Liverpool nonagenarian, recalls a crossing made with the intention of landing at Woodside shortly before the steam ferries came in. 'The tide was running very strong and the wind blowing hard and after four hours we managed to land at the Rock Perch, thankful that our lives had been spared.' We can believe him when he says that, at that time, thousands of Liverpool people had never been in Cheshire in their lives.

The steam ferries changed all this. The initiative in developing them came entirely from F. R. Price and other individuals on the Cheshire side, Liverpool corporation, who had bought up the old royal ferry rights, having no desire to aid in developments on the other side of the Mersey. The *Etna* came into service from Tranmere and the *Princess Charlotte* from Eastham shortly after steam was first introduced to the Mersey. By the 1830s all the ferries were steam operated and took not many more minutes to perform their journeys than their predecessors had taken hours. The number of ferries proliferated. Two more appeared on the Priory peninsula itself besides the Woodside ferry which was the historical descendant of the original monks' ferry. These were the Birkenhead ferry, encouraged by F. R. Price, owner of the Woodside ferry, and the so-called 'Monks' ferry, an impudent interloper whose career was cut short by legal action after not many years. There were ferries south of these at Tranmere, Rock Ferry, New Ferry and Eastham and north of

8 above *The east front of Bramall Hall.* *9* below *The gatehouse of Little Moreton Hall.*

them at Seacombe, Egremont and New Brighton. The passengers on the
New Brighton and Eastham ferries were mainly holiday-makers,
spending a day at the seaside or in Eastham woods. Most of the
passengers on the other routes were going about their daily business.

Such was the growth of the population on Merseyside that the opening
of the railway tunnel under the Mersey in 1886 did not diminish the
ferry traffic, which reached its peak in the years after the First World
War. Then 11-13 million passengers used the Woodside ferry annually
and about double that number the three Wallasey ferries. The heavy drop
in numbers came in the 1950s when the growth in private motoring made
the Mersey Road Tunnel, opened as long ago as 1933, a much more
formidable rival than the Railway Tunnel had ever been. Now the
enlarged entrance and the system of flyovers and one-way traffic lanes
that lead to it threaten to suck the indecisive or unknowledgeable motorist
in and spew him out on the Liverpool side of the river whether his
intention was to go over or not. As far as is known, no one suffered this
fate on the ferry boats. Some of these are now used for taking pleasure
trips up and down the river, but only the Woodside and Seacombe ferries
operate as such and the first is threatened with closure.

South of Birkenhead lies Bebbington, whose modern growth has
submerged the village Hawthorne loved so well with what he strangely
called, 'cockney residences from Liverpool'. Presumably he meant to
denote *English* suburban villas rather than American which, in fact, hardly
existed in his day. The church alone remains, its tower bearing one of the
three surviving medieval spires in Cheshire, and the interior containing
work from Norman times to the fifteenth century, with (for the Wirral)
surprisingly little Victorian restoration. But Bebbington is not all
suburbia. It contains two examples of the successful housing of factory
workers.

In 1853 Price's Patent Candle Company of Battersea established a
factory near the mouth of Bromborough Pool. They chose the site because
it was near Liverpool, from which came the palm oil that they needed,
because communications promised to be good and because there was space
for development. When the factory had been built, the remaining 50 acres
of the site were used for workers' cottages with parlour, kitchen and
scullery below, three bedrooms above, piped water and internal water
closets, the last an unheard of luxury in working-class housing in those

days. Land was set aside for allotments and later a school, a chapel and two hospitals were built. The scheme, although it was and has remained modest, has an honourable place in the story of the improvement of working-class housing. It was the first attempt in the north-west.

Further up the Pool a more ambitious scheme was begun in the 1880s. By careful experimenting and brilliant advertising, W. H. Lever had already made a fortune out of his Sunlight Soap factory at Warrington. Like the Candle Company he moved to Bromborough Pool because of the good communications and space for development. In addition to his great business ability and benevolent intentions, he had a strong artistic sensibility. He wanted his 'Port Sunlight' to be aesthetically pleasing and, as well as making his workers' cottages roomy and hygenic (although their water closets were external to begin with), he paid great attention to their layout. Communal gardens were included in the scheme from the beginning and impressive monuments and public buildings added later. Lever's long life and great wealth enabled him to expand and adapt Port Sunlight under a series of architects, each of whom was encouraged to build in the style of his day but in harmony with his predecessors. The present giant company of Unilever has maintained and developed the community.

South of Bebbington once lay the villages of Eastham, Childer Thornton and Whitby and the halls of Hooton and Poole, all inside the old Hundred of Wirral. But the Ship Canal, which continues right across north-west Cheshire, commences at Eastham, and all the rest have been swallowed up by Ellesmere Port, which is essentially a canal town. So treatment of the area is best reserved to the next chapter which deals with the canal country of north-west Cheshire. Because of his concentration on the Dee shore Leland omitted to mention the interior of the Wirral, and because of the claims of both Deeside and Merseyside, I have almost had to do the same. This is a pity, because there was, and still is, much charming and interesting country there. There are villages such as Willaston with its Elizabethan hall, its green with a mixture of houses from four centuries grouped round it, and its tall, brick windmill. The breezes of the Wirral made windmills far more common there than elsewhere in Cheshire. There is a fourteenth-century 'peel' or fortified tower house attached to the outbuildings of Brimstage Hall farm. The farm buildings of Storeton Hall farm have pieces in them of the great hall of Storeton, which was the first possession of the Stanleys in Cheshire before they acquired Hooton. The elder line of the Stanleys of Hooton were men of importance themselves in the affairs of the Wirral and the county at large for 500 years, but from them came the nationally more famous lines of the Stanley Earls of Derby and the Stanleys of Alderley. In Poulton Hall near by lives a descendant of the Launcelyns who were well established at Poulton before the Stanleys ever arrived in Cheshire. These families remind us that even in 'a piece of land between the seas', it was possible to lead a life that had nothing to do with the sea. None of them gained distinction as seafaring men, and they and their tenants seem to have been absorbed in farming and rural affairs in much the same way as those in the heart of Cheshire. Probably many of the farmers never went to the shore of the Mersey until the growth of Liverpool provided a market for the sale of potatoes and other vegetables, and it was found that the soil and climate of the Wirral were suitable for growing them. Then began the great century of market gardening in Wirral, and in those parts not built over it still flourishes. A drive along the new motorway, the M53, reveals in a flash that there still are such parts. For two-thirds of its course it seems to pass through meadows and woodland with only a hint of houses hidden behind the trees. It is only at the northern end of the peninsula that these are revealed, stretching across it almost unbroken from the Mersey to the Dee.

THREE

The North-West:
Canal Country

The Mersey, whose name means *river at the boundary,* was Cheshire's north-western boundary from the early days of the county until very recently. In the western half of the region, from Eastham to the Runcorn Gap, it is an estuary up to three miles broad and looking like an inland sea at high tide. A couple of miles above the Runcorn Gap, although tidal as far as Warrington, it becomes narrow and very winding and continues so until the confluence with the Irwell between Partington and Carrington. It was from prehistoric times on both a line of communication and a barrier, but in the last 300 years the ever increasing demands of industry and trade have eliminated it as an obstacle and utilised it and the region near it for swifter and swifter means of transport. So north-west Cheshire is crowded with river navigations and canals, railways, bridges of all sizes and descriptions and, in the latest phase, motor roads.

Archaeologists believe that the Mersey was one of the routes by which prehistoric cultures from northern Ireland pushed their way into the rest of Britain. The finding of several coin hoards suggests that Irish pirates found it useful during the decline of imperial Rome. The Norsemen at York and Dublin certainly utilised it as a line of communication; hence the building of *burhs* at Runcorn and Thelwall by Edward the Elder and Ethelfleda. But the superiority of the Dee as a waterway at this stage, the poverty of the region around the Mersey and the claims of fishermen and millers upon its waters seem to have brought it into almost complete disuse as a thoroughfare during the Middle Ages. Leland found Runcorn no more than a 'poore townlet by a salt creeke' and said significantly of Thelwall, 'now fishe garthes marre the haven'.

Despite the peat bogs and great marshes that persisted until modern times, from the thirteenth century on it became increasingly easy to get across this section of the Mersey. There were bridges on the main roads at Warrington and Crossford, fords, ferries and some minor bridges elsewhere. Cavaliers and Roundheads during the Civil War and the Jacobites in 1745 did not find it a major obstacle.

By 1745 commercial considerations were rapidly obliterating military ones. Already Liverpool merchants, combining with the new rock salt proprietors, had made the Weaver navigable to Northwich, while Warrington and Manchester merchants had done the same for the Mersey and its tributary, the Irwell, up to Manchester. In the first stages the channels were dredged and scoured, locks and some tow-paths for manhauling introduced. Later the tow-paths were adapted for use by horses and made continuous, and 'cuts' taken across the windings of the rivers. The greatest of the cuts was four miles long and, bypassing the old river mouth, took the Weaver Navigation into the Mersey at Weston Point. It is known as the Weaver 'canal' and, by the time it was completed, a real canal ran into the Mersey a mile or so to the north of it. This was the Duke of Bridgewater's Canal, which after running from the Duke's coal mines at Worsley via Stretford into Manchester, came out again from Stretford and crossed north Cheshire through Sale, Timperley, Dunham Massey, Lymm and Grappenhall. But, before running into the Mersey at Runcorn, it took a sharp turn southwards to Preston Brook, where it was joined by another canal, the Grand Trunk (now the Trent and Mersey) running up from Staffordshire. It was the interests of another coal proprietor, Lord Gower, and the pottery 'king', Josiah Wedgwood, that promoted this canal. That the two enterprises decided to join forces is not surprising. Bridgewater's sister had married Gower, their agents, John and Thomas Gilbert, were brothers, and the engineer for both canals was James Brindley, whom Thomas Gilbert had recommended to his brother. This powerful consortium were able to defeat in Parliament a scheme by east Cheshire landowners and manufacturers to build a canal to run from Stockport and Macclesfield into the Weaver Navigation.

The first seven miles of the canal, from Worsley into Manchester, took from 1758-61 to build. The remaining 20 miles across north Cheshire was not completed until 1777, five years after Brindley had died. If it had not been for the immediate success of the first part, the second might never have been completed, for the difficulties and delays were so great that they strained even the Duke's vast resources, and it was a loan from a London banking firm on the security of the Worsely-Manchester section which enabled the work to be continued.

Both Bridgewater and Grand Trunk Canals were very busy with goods traffic from the start, but the Bridgewater had a thriving passenger traffic as well. This was killed by the railways, but the introduction of steam instead of horses enabled the canals to keep a sizable amount of goods traffic throughout the nineteenth century and on into the twentieth. The railways came early to this part of Cheshire. The Grand Junction, linking the Liverpool and Manchester Railway with Birmingham, was opened in 1837, only seven years after the Liverpool and Manchester itself. The *Manchester Guardian* reporter on the opening run was amused at the panic of the cows in the nearby fields, compared with the phlegm which those alongside the Liverpool and Manchester line had already acquired. The new line swung south-west from Warrington before turning south-east and crossing the Weaver valley at Dutton on a stone viaduct of 20 arches, constructed by the engineer, Joseph Locke, and the wonder of its age. The *Guardian* reporter said (one would think truthfully) that, 'Though not favourably situated for seeing the whole of this stupendous work, the passengers very much admired the appearance of its solid masonry, suspended as it seemed over the valley below.'

Additional railway lines were added thick and fast in north-west Cheshire in the boom era of the railways. In 1850 the Chester and Birkenhead Railway ran a line through Helsby and Frodsham to join the Grand Junction (already absorbed into the London and North Western) at Higher Walton. In 1860 the Chester and Birkenhead was itself absorbed into the London and North Western which, four years later, decided to make a shorter and more convenient route to Scotland by bridging the quarter-mile Gap between Runcorn and Widnes. This it did with an iron bridge, which it called *Ethelfleda* to commemorate the fact that its stone piers on the Runcorn side sprang from the rock on which it is presumed the Saxon warrior 'lady' built her fort. The piers are crowned with appropriately warlike-looking turrets.

The railway lines, most of which ran north and south, did little to quieten Manchester's old complaints that Liverpool's dock dues were too heavy and the time taken to load and unload cargoes too long. The trade recession of the late 1870s, coupled with the success of the recently opened Suez Canal, led to a revival of the old scheme for a canal for ocean-going vessels to start from Manchester itself, and in 1882 the Ship Canal Company was formed among influential businessmen from Manchester and the towns round about. That this was a serious venture with some chance of success was admitted by *Punch* which came out with a cartoon entitled 'Manchester-sur-Mer, a Sea-ductive Prospect', and the Liverpool press which emitted cries of rage and alarm. 'The greatest bubble ever thrust upon the credulity of the British public since the South Sea Bubble', said one newspaper.

The company finally adopted the plan of Edward Leader Williams, formerly engineer to the Bridgewater Navigation and designer of the famous lift at Anderton near Northwich linking the Weaver Navigation and the Trent and Mersey Canal. This was for a freshwater canal with locks which, unlike the original suggestion of a tidal canal without locks, would ensure a sufficient depth of water at the Manchester end at all times. It was, of course, much more difficult and expensive to construct. Gales, floods, accidents caused by human error (130 people were killed and over 1,000 injured in the building of the canal), some miscalculations and the death of the original contractor delayed the work, and the funds ran out. The intervention of Manchester City Council, which loaned £5,000,000 to the company, saved the situation, so that when the Ship Canal was finally opened in 1894 it was in a very real sense Manchester's. It was busy from the start and has remained so, although all other canals in the country have seen their commercial traffic dwindle and disappear. But, oddly enough, it has never served the purpose for which its original promoters intended it, the cheap carriage of raw cotton into and finished cotton goods out of Manchester. The amount of cotton goods carried on the Canal was never large, even before the trade began to diminish.

When the Ship Canal was opened, the section that runs through or along the borders of Cheshire (all but eight of its 36 miles) began with Eastham Woods and ended with Carrington Moss. In the middle was the large and thinly inhabited stretch of Frodsham marshes. Only at Ellesmere Port, still a very small town of less than 4,000 inhabitants, Weston Point and Runcorn, and the southern outskirts of Warrington did it pass through districts that were urban and industrialised. The scene is very different now and this is basically the result of the opportunities offered by the existence of the canal. New industry, which began as a trickle after the First World War, swelled to a flood after the Second. The modest single oil refinery that started with one storage tank near the relics of the old monastic cell at Stanlow Point in 1922 has proliferated into refineries, allied chemical works and other industrial plants that entirely cover the western part of Frodsham Marsh and have spread on the other side of Ellesmere Port almost to Eastham. I.C.I. has vast works at Weston Point and the Runcorn Development Corporation has established new industrial estates which are as far east of the old town as Norton and Preston Brook. Warrington's industries south of the Mersey are mostly pre-Ship Canal and a great deal of the development in this area has been suburban, but Carrington and Partington have been converted from moss hamlets into busy offshoots of the petro-chemical industries.

So the north-west corner of Cheshire presents a panorama of mile after mile of the twentieth century: storage tanks, queer bulbous 'columns' for distillation and fractionisation, tall slender 'towers' for extraction and evaporation, metal inspection ladders and piping everywhere. Everything seems to be made of metal and gives off a kind of dull sheen. What comes out of the tall towers is whitey-grey and woolly. Anything further removed from the belching chimneys, soot and blackened brick of nineteenth-century industrialism can hardly be imagined. Yet even with the tallest towers there is pollution — what goes up must come down somewhere — and inhabitants of residential Helsby and Frodsham complain bitterly of smoke, smell, dust and noise floating over from new chemical works out on the marshes. Yet, at any rate, they do not obliterate all vegetation in the neighbourhood as their predecessors at Runcorn and Widnes used to do.

At night, without doubt, these modern industrial plants are beautiful, fully lighted and glittering like fairy palaces. To the layman they have a slightly sinister air, however, because although production is obviously going ahead all the time, no one appears to be there. A modern Nibelheim, uninhabited by Nibelungs. In fact, these factories do employ thousands of men; Shell, founder of the original refinery at Stanlow and still the company with the largest units there, has over 5,000 employees — but because of automation there is nothing like the number their nineteenth-century counterparts would have required. This fact, an advantage from the national as well as their own point of view during the labour shortage of the post-war years, does not carry the same attraction now.

Relics of previous centuries, even of pre-twentieth century industrialisation, have to be looked for in the area, although they do still exist. Bosdin Leech, a Manchester yarn merchant, one of the earliest and strongest promoters of the Canal and later its historian, admitted that 'it seemed almost desecration to invade' Eastham Woods, the 'Richmond of the Mersey', where Liverpool people came in thousands to picnic. A fragment of the woods still girdles the Victorian hotel and the remains of the jetty for the ferry, and is a pleasant green oasis from which to watch ships passing into the entrance to the Canal and the great oil dock just inside it. Much of the old Eastham village, another of Hawthorne's favourites, is still clustered round the church with its odd but attractive fourteenth-century spire, and an old country road with trees and hedges slips southward out of it. But parallel with this road runs a recent flyover with oil tanks in the background, and just round the other corner of the village is the A41's bypass with petrol stations and flat-roofed shops. It is very praiseworthy – the A41 traffic used to flow through the village – but so precarious that it almost makes one hold one's breath.

Ellesmere Port is a rarity among British towns: a canal port with not even a hamlet as an antecedent. Its name comes from the ambitious Ellesmere Canal scheme which was intended to link the Mersey, the Dee and the Severn. The length and difficulties of its routes and the drying up of capital because of the Napoleonic Wars caused the project to founder, but its first leg, the easy eight miles from Chester through the Backford Gap to the shores of the Mersey, was a success, although for reasons on which the promoters had not counted. This was the brisk passenger traffic between Chester and Liverpool. In Victorian times Ellesmere Port had a brief period as a modest seaside resort, ended by the coming of the Ship Canal in 1894. The opening of the Canal, the coming of the Shell oil refinery in 1922, of Bowater's Paper Company in the 1930s (when the London newspapers began printing northern editions), and Vauxhall Motors in the 1950s, have been the four landmarks in the town's recent development. It has swallowed up half a dozen hamlets around it and its population is over 60,000.

Telford's warehouses, a little of the original domestic housing and several later nineteenth-century streets are clustered round the exit of the canal from Chester into the Ship Canal. For the rest, Ellesmere Port is entirely a twentieth-century town. The Civic Hall, library, municipal offices and shopping precinct were all built between 1954 and 1970. They may not be unusually distinguished or adventurous architecturally, but they are bright, clean, spacious and convenient. The indoor swimming pool, opened by the Prime Minister in 1969 and large enough for national championships to be held in it, is in itself a considerable monument to civic pride. Although its recent borough has gone, Ellesmere Port is now the centre for one of the new county districts.

Eastwards is a relic of a much more distant past, the little village of Ince. Its name is derived from the Celtic *ynys,* an island. Once it was islanded by the marshes, now by oil storage tanks. Like Eastham, it is a breathtaking survival. The church, old village square and a few lush meadows with cattle grazing are screened on their little hill from the rows and rows of storage tanks by a fringe of great trees.

On the edge of the village are two ruined buildings of great sandstone blocks, part of the late medieval hall of the manor of Ince. The lord of the manor was the abbot of St Werburgh's, Chester, one of whose other residences, at Saighton south of Chester, has been restored as a modern residence by the Dukes of Westminster. Ince had some importance and a modest prosperity in the Middle Ages and later because it was at the Cheshire end of a ford across the Mersey coming from Hale in Lancashire. Like the fords over the Dee at Hawarden this one was much subject to shiftings of the sands, and knowledge that was local and up-to-date was essential for a safe crossing. It was perforce much used by the royalists in the Civil War because the parliamentarians were usually in control of the Mersey bridges.

Frodsham, nestling under the bluff of Overton Hill, has a recorded history going back to late Saxon times. As it is close to several prehistoric forts and on the A56 it is likely that the settlement there is still older. For the A56 follows what was probably the route from Deva to the Roman fort and industrial settlement at the Wilderspool crossing of the Mersey near Warrington. Frodsham was one of the principal manors of Edwin, the last Saxon earl of Mercia, of the Norman earls of Chester and finally of the Crown. It reared quantities of sheep and cattle, had fisheries and a windmill as well as a watermill, and strove (not always successfully) to drain part of the marshes and keep them from flooding by means of dikes and a sluice. The church at Frodsham is mentioned in Domesday Book, and in the present building halfway up Overton Hill are portions of a Norman nave and clerestory.

In the thirteenth century Frodsham had an unusual lord. He was Dafydd ap Gruffudd, who was granted the manor by Edward I for aiding the English against his brother, Prince Llywelyn, with whom he had quarrelled. When he tired of English domination and was the main instigator of the Second Welsh War, he suffered the terrible punishment of being hung, drawn and quartered. In the eighteenth century Frodsham had an unusual vicar too, who incurred the everlasting curse of all lovers of Shakespeare's birthplace. He was Francis Gastrell and he purchased the poet's New Place at Stratford, leaving his parish to live in it. He first of all cut down the mulberry tree, as it attracted sightseers who annoyed him, and then pulled down the house itself rather than pay the poor rate which the Stratford corporation demanded of him.

The road through Frodsham, probably the original cause of its existence, threatened to destroy the town in the post Second World War years. Because the A56 was the nearest and most convenient route north from the new industrial belt on the Cheshire shores of Merseyside, great lorries thundered through the main street day and night. Now because of the relief given by the new M56, it is possible once again to cross over the old, broad, tree-lined High Street without agitation and saunter along it in peace. This restoration of their dignity and sanity to many old villages and country towns must, at least, be put to the social credit of motorways.

The broad valley of the Weaver, very busy and industrialised below Frodsham, is very peaceful and rural above it, despite the presence of two great monuments of England's transport revolution, the Grand Junction viaduct at Dutton and the cuts and locks on the river navigation to the east of it. The Lower Weaver could almost be called the Valley of the Departed, for in it in Tudor and Stuart times were the mansions of three of the wealthiest and most influential families in the county, the Savages, the Duttons and the Astons. The pathetic remains of Rocksavage, whose modernity, being brick-built and with extensive gardens, so excited the admiration of William Webb in the early seventeenth century, are lost among the Weston Point I.C.I. works, the housing development at

Runcorn New Town and an interchange of the M56. The timber mansion of the Duttons was bought up by a whisky magnate in the 1930s, and removed to Sussex. Aston Hall has gone also. But there does remain the charming church of Aston-by-Sutton, standing almost alone beside a quiet country road. The chancel is late seventeenth-century (there is evidence that Vanbrugh may have had a hand in designing it), the nave early Georgian. In it are monuments to Sir Thomas Aston and his son, Sir Willoughby. Sir Thomas was the royalist general in command against Brereton in Cheshire at the beginning of the war. After two defeats, following which he appeared in Chester having lost his entire army, he was removed south. But of his loyalty and gallantry there was no doubt and he died fighting for King Charles. He was more outstanding as the first royalist who said and wrote openly in the days just before the Civil War, that to destroy the bishops was to threaten both the monarchy and the social order. This was a far from popular line at the time even with members of his own side, but after the disasters of the war most of them came round to adopting it. His father's fate and the huge fines imposed on the family fortune by Parliament made Sir Willoughby a more discreet and pliable type, although equally active. He produced eight sons and thirteen daughters and kept a voluminous diary, now in the archives of Liverpool Library. His conduct when the Duke of Monmouth visited Cheshire produced an interview with a deeply suspicious Judge Jeffreys, then Chief Justice of Chester, but Sir Willoughby, although he was undoubtedly dabbling in Whiggery, was able to cover his tracks.

At the end of two miles of docks and wharfs beside the Ship Canal is Bridgewater House, erected by the Duke as a temporary home while the Bridgewater Canal was being finished. It stands starkly alone where Brindley's ten locks used to bring the otherwise lockless canal down to the level of the Mersey. It is, in a way, a revelation of the Duke's enormous wealth with standards to match. For it was put up when the Duke was supposed to be saving every penny for the sake of the canal and living rough. Yet it is three storeys high with a basement, five bays wide and deeper than it is wide. Peter the Great was content with residences half the size when St Petersburg was being built.

At any rate, this is where the strange trio met who planned and executed the construction of the canal. The Duke had forsaken the world of high society into which he was born, perhaps because of unsuccessful love affairs, but more likely because he found increasing his vast wealth by developing a modern means of communication infinitely more interesting. Brindley was not so illiterate that he had to carry all his calculations in his head, as tradition has alleged. His spelling was individual, but would have passed muster in all ages prior to his own, which had regularised spelling. There is evidence that he often drew plans. But he *was* the son of a Derbyshire labourer who owed little to formal education and almost everything to his powers of practical application, observation and imagination. Through working in watermills up and down the Cheshire-Derbyshire-Staffordshire borders he had acquired a great reputation there as a 'wizard' in hydraulics before he ever gained national fame as a builder of canals. He appears to have been entirely unselfconscious, and able to convey his enthusiasm to others and explain his ideas simply and graphically to the layman. These gifts made him acceptable in all walks of society.

John Gilbert, the Duke's agent, appears almost colourless in his normality besides the other two, but there is no doubt that he was hardworking, persevering and efficient. Some recent writers have thought that part of the credit usually given to Brindley for the surveying of the Bridgewater Canal ought to go to him, but such evidence as there is is not conclusive.

There is something of nineteenth-century industrial Runcorn in the terraces of houses that run almost under the arches of the two great bridges across to Widnes. If Hawthorne thought Chester and Bebbington had no parallel in the United States, he thought Runcorn had not either and was glad of it: 'Two or three tall manufacturing chimneys, with a pennant of black smoke from each; . . . a church or two and a meagre uninteresting, shabby, brick-built town, . . . with irregular streets, not village-like but paved and looking like a dwarfed stunted city. We cannot conceive, in America, of anything so unpicturesque as this English town.'

Since Hawthorne wrote in the 1850s the great bridges and the Ship Canal have removed some of the 'meagreness' and lack of interest from Runcorn. Their existence has also added to the industries and prospects of employment in the town, and, together with the thinly populated hinterland to the east of it, has led to its being chosen as the site for a new town, to house an overspill from Liverpool and eventually support a population of 100,000. The master plan of the Runcorn Development

Corporation, as yet only half-completed, is certainly bold, imaginative and all-embracing. The new centre is fully two miles south-east of the old town centre, and has the ancient village of Halton, set with its ruined castle on a conical hill, as a focal point. 'Communities' of 8,000 inhabitants are being grouped round it. They are housed in ranges of low-storeyed concrete flats and courtyard houses, which are set in parkland, have local shops and primary schools attached, and are on a figure-of-eight bus route whose intersection is a 'shopping city' just south of Halton Hill. This is completely enclosed and, besides shops, has restaurants, bars and a multi-storey car park. A hospital, technical college, and cultural and commercial buildings are to follow in the same area. North and south of the town two large industrial estates are being built up, and a very up-to-date flavour has been imparted to one of these by the appearance in it of Yoshida K.K., a Japanese firm with world-wide ramifications, specialising in the making of zippers.

One must be grateful to the planners for their decision to preserve Halton entire in the centre of the new scheme, but the community flats creeping up round it have inevitably destroyed the dramatic outline that used to rise up out of the surrounding plain, making it look more like an Italian medieval village than an English one. Actually what crowns the hill is the slender bell turret of Gilbert Scott's Victorian church; original fragments of the castle are too scanty even to indicate its shape (engravings tell us it must have been a shell-keep) and none of the cluster of old buildings below it date further back than late Tudor times. Yet the set of the steep streets and the whole atmosphere is medieval.

The lords of Halton from Norman times on were constables of Chester and, therefore, the commanders of the shire's forces under the earl. They played a major part in the wars with the Welsh. One, certainly, died leading the vanguard when a royal army invading North Wales was ambushed, and two are credited with last minute – in one case, miraculous – rescues of the earl from surprise attacks by the Welsh. Like the earls, the constables were men of national as well as local importance. They led forces to the Crusades, defended royal castles in Normandy against the king of France and one of them, Henry de Lacy, was regent of England in all but name after the death of Edward I. Eventually castle and constableship passed to the Dukes of Lancaster and then, in the person of Henry Bolingbroke who became King Henry IV, to the crown of

Cheshire

England. That is why the Castle Hotel, built in the early eighteenth century from stones taken from the castle, was once the Duchy Court House.

North of Halton lay Norton Priory, during the Middle Ages a house of the Augustinian Canons, after the Dissolution a Tudor hall, finally a Georgian mansion with Victorian additions. The owners were the Brookes, a family of ancient descent from the Nantwich area, who did not become prominent until Tudor times but then lasted until the twentieth century as men of first importance in county affairs. Several of them represented it in Parliament. At length rising costs and the increasingly industrial nature of the surroundings caused them to pull the house down and move south. The grounds became a tangled wilderness until the Runcorn Development Corporation took them over to make into a public park. With great foresight they appointed a professional archaeologist to their staff and he carried out on the old priory one of the most thorough excavations of a monastic site ever made in Britain. The results are now open to the public and, although there is little above foundation level, what has been laid bare is so complete that anyone who wishes to study the layout of monastic buildings *in situ* should pay a visit. The one surviving building is the undercroft to the west of the cloister, which was converted into an entrance hall for the house in the nineteenth century. It contains the finest Norman doorway in Cheshire with a Victorian replica alongside it. A small temporary museum has been opened on the site to display finds and information and it is hoped that a much larger permanent one will follow, where it will be possible to display the whole of the very large collection of mosaic and inlaid tiles which were discovered.

The suburbs of Warrington have now extended a full mile south of the Ship Canal and not only submerged the interesting Roman site at Wilderspool but reached the old village of Grappenhall, which is now another of Cheshire's many islands of the past. Its village street still has cobbles, and in the late medieval church is Cheshire's only complete window of medieval glass. It is a jumble of pieces taken out of the original stone frame and fitted into a later one none too skilfully, but the figures of five saints and Mary Magdalene are apparent, and there is no mistaking the splendid glow of the colours.

In the few miles between the outskirts of Warrington and the outskirts

10 above Old houses in Prestbury; the timber-framed bank, once the vicarage, dates from the fifteenth century. 11 below War memorial and Lady Lever Art Gallery, Port Sunlight.

of Manchester are some of the most delightful stretches of the Bridgewater Canal, rich pastures and grazing cows providing an improbable foreground to the backcloth of industrial Lancashire which forms the northern horizon. Nowadays the Lymm and Sale Cruising Clubs take full advantage of this, but sailing along the canal just for pleasure was not unknown in its early days. In 1789 a grand Middlesex lady, the wife of an admiral, visited the barbarous north-west. She found nothing to her liking except a ride along the Duke's canal from Manchester to Warrington: 'A very agreeable novelty to my young folks. We passed over 9 bridges and under 23.' The Manchester textile workers poured out along it in Whit Week when the earl of Stamford threw Dunham Park open to them. A vivid description of such a visit is contained in Mrs Gaskell's short story, *Libby Marsh's Three Eras,* recently republished by the Lancashire and Cheshire Antiquarian Society under the title of *Life in Manchester, 1847.*

The canal passes by Lymm, an ancient village built on the sides of a rocky ravine. The steepness of the street — known appropriately as Eagle Brow — which descends into the old market place caused some re-routing in the coaching age and the new turnpike, now the A56, was diverted south of the village. Although housing has spread in all directions and linked with neighbouring villages, this has preserved the centre of Lymm intact and, with it, Lymm's identity and its pride. For, although commuters have come in both from Manchester and Warrington, they have merged in with the older community and nowhere in Cheshire is interest in its past and desire that continuty should not be broken stronger.

When Dunham Park and its attendant villages, the domain of the Earl of Stamford and his predecessors, the Booths, are reached, the Bridgewater Canal turns northwards and follows its mightier neighbour, the Ship Canal into Manchester, the town which was the principal cause of the existence of both of them.

12 above *Chester cathedral from the south; the detached bell tower in the foreground is a very recent addition. 13* below *Lower Peover church.*

FOUR

Northern Cheshire or Southern Manchester?

'Well, Jack, and where art thou bound to?'
'Dunham.'
'Why, what an old-fashioned chap thou be'est. They grandad afore thee went to Dunham; but thou wert always a slow coach. I'm off to Alderley – me and my missus.'

This dialogue between two textile workers in a Manchester courtyard sometime in the 1840s (taken from Mrs Gaskell's *Libby Marsh's Three Eras*) marks the faint beginning of Manchester's great Cheshire dormitory, although it was not the workers who came to live on the delectable slopes of Bowdon Hill or Alderley Edge. The recently opened Birmingham and Manchester Railway had a stopping place close to the Edge and was prepared to run cheap excursions there during Whit Week, while Lord Stanley of Alderley threw open to the public its most picturesque spots. Those workers able to afford it took the opportunity. The others (Jack had several children while his mate had none) continued to make the cheaper excursion by canal to Dunham Park, which the co-operation of the Canal Duke and the Earl of Stamford had made possible half a century before.

The correspondence of the female members of the Stanley family show us the next stage. A 'rail-roader' (Mr Waddington, Deputy Chairman of the Birmingham and Manchester) called on Lord Stanley to gain permission for a special reserved day on the Edge for the families of Manchester's manufacturers, merchants and railway directors. If it had been left to the Stanley ladies the permission is unlikely to have been granted. It was they who had coined the phrase 'Cottentots' for this new society, and Lady Stanley complained that it was much more annoying to have them about on the Edge than the operatives, 'as one can neither handcuff nor great dog them if they are intrusive or offensive'. Nevertheless, after some demurring and delaying, permission does seem to have been granted.

Desire to flee from the grimy towns that the Industrial Revolution had created, if only for short breaks or the non-working part of the day, was certainly growing, and Manchester was, by common consent, the town which represented the Revolution in all its most horrifying aspects. 'This great, nasty manufacturing town' (John Byng), 'this foul drain' (De Tocqueville), 'the chimney of the world . . . the entrance to hell realised' (General Sir Charles Napier), 'sooty Manchester . . . built upon the infinite abysses' (Carlyle), are a handful of descriptions from distinguished visitors. Natives would be less likely to overdramatise its disadvantages, but the teachers of the Sunday Schools who brought their scholars to the Edge in Whit Week 1843, despite a wet and windy day, were voluble to their benefactors on the pleasure all had had 'in seeing such scenery and breathing such pure air'. A young man from the Cottentot class itself, after a month in Altrincham recuperating from an illness, spent his final hours there walking in Dunham Park and recorded in his diary that he could not enjoy it, 'for thinking that it was the last time I should enjoy its fragrant shades which have given me so much pleasure and I was going to leave it for a nasty, dirty, smoky town'.

By the end of the 1840s the further spread of the railways and the willingness of some of the landlords to sell off part of their estates gave the wealthiest Cottentots the opportunity of enjoying these delights more permanently. The Stanleys were determined to preserve the Edge itself, but the De Traffords, who did not live in the district, sold off land for villas on the lower slopes and the plain westwards. So arose the new community of Alderley Edge, where before there had been only Chorley, a late medieval-cum-Elizabethan hall with surrounding farms and cottages. At Dunham, too, the Earls of Stamford became non-resident and, while they retained complete control of the Park and all their estates west of the Manchester-Chester road, they were prepared to sell off their extensive property in Bowdon, Altrincham and western Hale. To take advantage of the inevitable demand, the 'railroaders' launched the first commuter line in the north-west, the Manchester and South Junction and Altrincham Railway in 1849. By the 1860s the slopes of Bowdon, like those of Alderley Edge, were covered with villas. Then the Cheshire Midland Railway, running a line through from Manchester to the mid-Cheshire salt fields, placed a halt in Hale. Leo Grindon, an amateur botanist who wrote a popular series on country rambles which could be made through using the railways out of Manchester, drew attention to the charm of the quiet farms and cottages of this region and even more to the tranquillity and seclusion of the Bollin Valley at its doors, 'the only one so near Manchester where nature lives in unmolested originality'. What with the new railway and his writings it did not long remain in this state. Partly because it was possible for children to paddle and even to bathe in it, the Bollin came to replace both Dunham Park and Alderley Edge as the favourite nearby picnic spot for Manchester work people, and the trek to it did not die out until well after the Second World War. In addition, the trickle of villas which had begun to spread from Hale railway station in the 1860s increased to a flood in the 1880s and 1890s. 'They all go to Heaven or Hale', said a Manchester clergyman of his dwindling congregation at this time.

This second great wave of commuters had brought out professional people of not quite the same great wealth as some of the early Cottentots, but still prosperous enough. A writer at the end of the century describes the atmosphere of Bowdon:

> 'Its air of being well-to-do is almost aggressive. Everyone seems bright and busy and the wealth of Manchester flits gaily through the roads on the backs of the wives and sisters and aunts and cousins of its magnates and in the luxurious perambulators and expensive clothing of its babies.'

These commuters had come as far away from their daily place of work as their money and the speed of the trains would allow them to do, to a pleasant river valley and wooded heights overlooking the Cheshire plain, from which Manchester appeared only as a cloud of smoke 'far, far away in the distance'. The part of Cheshire north of these early suburbs was less attractive because flatter − often old moss or moor-land − and nearer to Manchester and Stockport. Therefore it filled up more slowly. At Sale,

Timperley, Cheadle, Cheadle Hulme and Northenden new buildings at first hugged the railway lines. Right in the centre, where only one railway line ran across its northern end, a great band of untouched country stretched almost from the Mersey to the Bollin. Just south of the Mersey lay the property of the Tattons of Wythenshawe who were still in residence, and in the depths of their parkland the invisible trains did no more than prick up the ears of the hares and rabbits for a few seconds with their passing whistles. Further south round about Ringway there were great farms on the fringe of the Egerton of Tatton estates which stretched away unbroken to Tatton Park itself.

In fact, a great deal of prosperous agriculture and horticulture went on in the region, even around and among the new suburbs, because of the huge market that lay at its door. The Timperley area supplied potatoes, onions, carrots and, later, beetroots for the Manchester market. On the 1907 six-inch Ordnance Survey map of Hale, almost all the spaces between the newly-built streets are occupied by nurseries. At the same period T. A. Coward noted that in Gatley, only just across the Mersey from the houses that by this time stretched unbroken from the centre of Manchester, 'Small farms and cottages have their fields cut up into squares wherein are growing onions, thyme, parsley, and herbs and great patches of pinks, primroses and daffodils in their various seasons.'

It was development after the First World War, the motor bus and the cheap private car and the local authority housing estate, that finally filled up the gaps. Manchester corporation bought up the Tatton lands and itself planned and developed the great Wythenshawe housing estate there. Private housing began to spring up in places well away from convenient railway stations, parts of Sale and Ashton-on-Mersey, Hale Barns, parts of Bramhall. Much of it was for a class whose means were well below that of all the nineteenth-century commuters. By the 1960s Manchester stretched to the Bollin, the line of houses broken only by the Mersey and its swampy valley. In April 1974, as in northern Wirral, administrative recognition was given to this physical fact and the whole region, with the exception of Wilmslow and Alderley Edge, passed out of Cheshire into Greater Manchester. Wilmslow and Alderley could claim that they lie further south than any of the other suburbs and that there is more ground unbuilt on between them and the old Manchester than elsewhere. Complicated financial and social reasons had more weight than these facts, however, and there is no doubt that in their present form they are as much the creation of commuting from Manchester as any of the other places that have now become part of Greater Manchester.

In fact, the pattern of commuting is now a great deal more complicated than it used to be, and by no means confined to a daily trek in and out of Manchester in the area covered by this chapter. The establishment of light industry in it, the proliferation of shops, offices, schools, colleges and research centres all over it, have resulted in a frenzied cross traffic, travelling east and west instead of north and south every week-day morning and evening. It is entirely composed of private cars, as no rail and few bus services cover such routes, and much of it pours along highly unsuitable country by-roads. In addition, fast reliable cars and good roads have made commuting into Manchester possible from places well outside the built-up areas. Some come in from Tarporley and even Nantwich, and the most select of commuting communities is now said to be at Prestbury over a dozen miles from Manchester – with a belt of open country in between – and barely three from Macclesfield. Finally there is a new commuting dimension. The chairman of a great international combine, living at Alderley Edge, has said that the real centre of an enterprise like his is always London and that he might have to spend two or three days a week there. The throng of cars waiting at Wilmslow station every evening for the inter-city trains from London reveals that he is far from being alone.

This is the so-called 'swell-belt', but the 'swellest' parts of the belt have always been on its outer edge and there have been since its creation parts that have never been swell. In the period just before the great change it was a region of small farmers and cottagers, adding to their modest incomes by tanning and spinning and weaving in their own homes. Scattered about were a number of water-powered mills, spinning cotton, linen and, occasionally, silk. Attached to each community were blacksmiths, wheel-wrights and tailors, the latter often semi-peripatetic. When the railways and commuters came, they brought with them bricklayers and carpenters, coachmen and gardeners, shopkeepers, railway workers. New working-class communities appeared at old centres, like the New Town, mysteriously nicknamed 'Calais', at Altrincham. With the passing of the water-power age, the isolated mills tended to disappear, but eventually new industries moved out of the overcrowded industrial areas of Manchester bringing new workers with them. Again, Altrincham's light engineering works at Broadheath are a case in point. Finally there came Manchester's 'overspill' estates.

In all this modern sea of bricks and mortar, it may seem inevitable that what has gone before will be utterly submerged. Yet certain landmarks remain clearly visible and others are discoverable by the persistent. Bowdon parish church still stands, as it has stood since Domesday Book, 'conspicuous far off, situate upon a hill'. The present building was put up in 1858, in response to the demand from the new Cottentot community for something more commodious and representative of their wealth and pride than the old late medieval church. W. H. Brakspear, the architect, gave them something that answered their demands and was worthy of the natural beauty and antiquity of the site. Its nave and aisles are spacious and its west tower dignified, its carving well executed throughout. Inside are many relics of the parish's long past. The camber beam roofs of the two aisles belonged to the previous church. There are monuments to eighteenth-century Booths and effigies of seventeenth-century Breretons of Ashley, and a fourteenth-century knight of the Baguley family. (Ashley and Baguley and other places more remote were in the huge medieval parish of Bowdon.) Finally there are fragments preserved in the north chancel from the fourteenth-century, Norman and Saxon churches.

For a similar impression of continuity the searcher must go to Dunham Park, on the far side of the Chester-Manchester road from the conurbation and still in an entirely rural setting. At Dunham lived and still live the family whose group of tiny manors were the distant antecedents of the present suburbs. From the Masseys who were there at the time of Domesday, the manor passed by marriage in the early fifteenth century to a junior branch of the Booths of Barton-on-Irwell. From the Booths it passed, once more by marriage, in mid-eighteenth century to the Earls of Stamford, already noted as the Grey family who were very close to the throne in Yorkist and early Tudor times. The house was built by the last Booth, George, second Earl of Warrington. He was an unheroic eighteenth-century gentleman, whose favourite text was 'But if any provide not for his own, ... he hath denied the faith', which he acted up to by arranging a marriage with a London heiress whom he had never seen and only just heard of. However, he gained some reputation as a patriot by planting thousands of great trees in the park. (This was a time when there was alarm that shortage of timber would threaten the 'wooden walls'.) He also earned the blessings of generations of later visitors to the park, from John Byng in 1790, who was vitriolic about the house but loved 'the melancholy shade of great boughs', to the hundreds who now walk through every weekend, summer or winter.

An engraving exists of the great Elizabethan house which the last Booth pulled down (one of the first brick mansions in Cheshire) and there is a survival of its day in the delightful little brick mill in front of the Hall. Both were built round about the time of the Armada by Sir George Booth, the first baronet, who lived long enough to see England a Commonwealth. As head of the Cheshire bench of justices and a venerable and respected figure in the county, he made an unavailing but very courageous attempt to halt the coming of the Civil War to Cheshire. He had a meeting called on Knutsford Heath where a 'Remonstrance' was put out, afterwards signed by thousands of people, which denounced as enemies of their country all who fomented the divisions between King and Parliament by proclaiming that they were 'for the King' or 'for the Parliament'. His grandson, Sir George the Younger, nevertheless fought for the Parliament, but was excluded from the Commons for opposing the trial of Charles I. He protested throughout Cromwell's rule against military interference with Parliament and, after Cromwell's death, raised a revolt to restore not so much Charles II as the old government by King, Lords and Commons. It is sometimes said that he changed sides. In fact, no man was more consistent; it was not he but the sides that changed. His son, Henry, the first Earl of Warrington, took his support of Parliament to even greater lengths. Constantly denouncing royal encroachments on its powers, he narrowly escaped execution for complicity in Monmouth's rising and played a major part in placing William of Orange on the throne. Portraits survive of all these Booths, whose active careers were interwoven with the main strands of English history for over a century. Those of the two Sir Georges are in Dunham Massey Hall itself (not open to the public), that of the first Earl of Warrington in Adlington, that of the second in Tatton.

Bowdon has no pre-nineteenth century buildings; Hale a few, both brick and timber, scattered about. Undoubtedly its most interesting one is the Unitarian Chapel in Hale Barns, built in 1723. It became Unitarian in the mid-eighteenth century like many of the other early chapels of the old Non-conformity. Its outside has been more altered than the parallel and slightly older chapels at Knutsford, Macclesfield and Dean Row, Wilmslow. But the interior with its box pews grouped round the pulpit and its splendid sounding board is little changed. Furthermore, its congregation is older than the chapel and has a continuous history going back to the Civil War, when zealous Puritans took possession of the little chapel of ease a mile away at Ringway, a building long since pulled down. Their remoteness, their own determination and the sympathy of some local landlords enabled the Puritans to remain in Ringway, despite the stringent laws against Non-conformist meetings passed by Parliament after the Restoration. Eventually the Revolution of 1688 and the Toleration Act that followed it enabled them to build their own chapel. It is one of the many evils of the present soaring inflation that it is almost impossible for such a congregation, although still vigorous, to obtain and support a minister, even in a chapel so interesting and delightful as this one.

Bowdon's nineteenth-century buildings, though unremarkable individually, are pleasant and significant as a group, an early commuters' paradise, set amid leafy avenues overlooking the Cheshire plain. The group is vulnerable now and Bowdon's Civic Society has to be constantly on guard to prevent its break-up. The rateable values of the large houses are high and the lack of servants makes them difficult to run. It is tempting to sell off the huge gardens as building plots. Hale's 'villas', being later than Bowdon's, tend not to be so large, and contain an outstanding small group designed at the turn of the century by the Manchester architect Edgar Wood, whose work was treated with interest and respect in Germany and Scandinavia. Wood's houses, all in or near the centre of Hale Road, range from half-timbered and pargetted Halecroft to flat-roofed, quadrant-shaped Royd House (the child of his old age). But most of them belong to his Arts and Crafts period and, although they are not direct imitations, have a pleasant flavour of the vernacular brick houses of the late sixteenth and seventeenth centuries.

For a town which had its first charter about 1290 (a fourteenth-century re-issue still survives), Altrincham has a quite staggering lack of buildings of any antiquity. The centre was rebuilt at the end of the nineteenth century and is being rebuilt again now with similar completeness. It is true that the town has never had much of a reputation for impressive appearance. Leland was rude about it in Tudor times, Sir Peter Leicester in the mid-seventeenth century and the Municipal Corporations Report in the early nineteenth century. Yet there have been those who found it pleasant enough. John Owen, the Manchester antiquary, lovingly sketched its cottages and inns and was desolated when they were pulled down. Another writer said that in spring time it was smothered in apple blossom, while De Quincey has left an unforgettable childhood impression of the profusion and gaiety of its market. That tradition, at any rate, has not been lost. The market, which was first recorded about the time of the granting of the charter, is still in the open air, still thronged with purchasers and full of vitality.

There was no town of Sale before the railway came. There was only a scattering of cottages near the Old and New Halls of the Masseys of Sale, a junior branch of the Masseys of Dunham. Both halls stood near the Mersey where the northern outskirts of the modern town are. On the main Chester-Manchester road, half-a-mile before Crossford Bridge over the Mersey was reached, was the little hamlet of Cross Street. On the far side of the road a more sizable village clustered round the parish church of Ashton-on-Mersey. The coaching and canal age brought a few more inhabitants to Cross Street and certainly put Sale on the travellers' map, for Brindley's embankment across the Moor was one of the principal wonders of the Bridgewater Canal until the railway line and the houses spoilt its outline. 'A most beautiful piece of water', wrote an early nineteenth-century writer, 'being so straight for two miles, that you look through three bridges and at its extent stands the parish church of Boden'.

The railway station of 1849 was placed on the edge of the Moor (by this time enclosed) and the new town grew up round it. A town hall, built in 1914, and a shopping street running from the station to the main road have not made much of a centre for Sale which, architecturally, is a sprawling and rather amorphous town. The community that has grown up there, however, has been vigorous enough and perhaps tighter knit and more conscious of itself than communities in the plushier districts of Bowdon and Hale. From among its many activities Sale Choir has won national recognition and so has Sale Rugby Club, although surrounded by a region that has scarcely taken Rugby Union Football to its bosom.

The central band of the commuter region is mostly occupied by the Wythenshawe Estate and Ringway Airport, both enterprises begun by

Manchester City Council in the inter-war years and controlled by them. Before this it was an area with two ancient manorial halls (Baguley and Wythenshawe), one parish church with village attached (Northenden), and no other settlement of any size. Much of it was unenclosed; peat mosses, moors and little greens with small farms and cottages lying on their edges.

On the eastern side of the commuter belt Cheadle parish church has miraculously survived both the Victorian urge for bigger and better places of worship, and the modern development which has turned the old High Street into a thoroughfare for the unending traffic in and out of Stockport. (It has become rather quieter since the new motorway appeared.) The main fabric of the church dates from a renewal which took place in the first half of the sixteenth century. Tower and nave have battlemented parapets, and inside there is a splendid camber beam roof and wooden screens of exquisite workmanship in the Savage and Brereton chapels. There is evidence of a much earlier church on the site and an eleventh-century Saxon cross was discovered in the churchyard.

Nearness to the waters of the Mersey brought several mills to Cheadle at the end of the eighteenth century, and nearness to Stockport and Manchester prolonged them into the age of steam. The 1841 census shows an amazing mixture of farmers and farm labourers, workers in cotton and silk mills and calico print works, handloom weavers of both cotton and silk, dyers and bleachers. The railway did not come through until the 1860s and it was not until some time after that that the tide of commuters submerged industry. On Cheadle Heath over towards Stockport this has never happened. Southwards the countryside survived much longer too, and there are still patches of greenery between Cheadle and Cheadle Hulme, and Cheadle and Bramhall.

Bramhall is very much twentieth-century suburbia. Previously the Hall, owned by a junior branch of the great Davenport family, had only a tiny hamlet by it. As a result of a remarkable series of fortunate circumstances the Hall is still there, excellently preserved under the local authority and open to the public, and with so much of the old park around it that in summer, when the leaves are on the trees, it is possible to imagine that the whole setting is still deep in the country. In addition, because of the generosity of the descendants of the Bramhall Davenports, now resident in the south, and other branches of the family, many of the family portraits and other furniture are now back in the Hall on loan. The south wing dates from the fifteenth century, but most of the rest of the Hall was rebuilt or refashioned in late Elizabethan times. It must be accounted the first fortunate circumstance that Sir William Davenport who did the rebuilding, although he was knighted and in 1604 served as sheriff, was not sufficiently wealthy nor in touch with London and the court to wish to build in fashionable brick, as his fellow squires had done or were doing at Dunham, Rocksavage, Brereton and Dorfold. So there is a wealth of timber framing throughout, quatrefoils in wood and plaster outside, moulded beams and doorcases inside. There are many other treasures also, the plaster ceiling and overmantel of the withdrawing room, the medieval glass in the chapel, the heraldic glass of the great hall, the tapestry of the Davenport family tree.

The son of the rebuilder of the Hall, another William, left memoranda, fortunately preserved and now in the City Archives at Chester. They give a glimpse of what life was like during the Civil War for a squire whose principal wish was to be left alone. William tried to raise his tenants for the King at the outset of the war, failed (it would not appear he tried very hard) and later supplied his quota for the more dominant parliamentarians. As the war swayed back and forwards in the area, troops of both sides quartered themselves at the Hall and took livestock (mostly horses) and sometimes household utensils as well. In the end William was fined £750 by the parliamentarian sequestrators for aiding the King! His presence at Bramhall and his pliability did not go quite unrewarded, however. The Hall suffered no serious damage, which it would have done had he taken sides enthusiastically or simply forsaken it for a safer area. His neutrality is the more surprising in that his memoranda reveal him to have been quite interested in national politics in pre-war times and not without a standpoint. He was obviously critical of Charles I's government — its financial exactions, its 'popish' taint, its humiliating foreign policy. Yet this did not cause him, when the time came, to stand up and be counted among the followers of Pym and Hampden, who were calling for constitutional limitations upon the royal power.

Two of his neighbours, however, Thomas Stanley of Alderley and Sir William Brereton of Handforth, did just this. Handforth Hall still stands, but after a prolonged period without occupants, more damaged by vandals than it ever was by the forays of passing royalists. It is to be hoped that reoccupation will at least restore it to its condition of some years back. The building was undoubtedly larger in Sir William's day and perhaps quadrangular. Its porch and that of Adlington, which is inside a quadrangle, are similar and have a similar type of inscription on them. This is not surprising because Urian Brereton, Sir William's great-grandfather, built Handforth Hall in 1562; his son-in-law, Thomas Legh, built Adlington in 1581. Sir William's line died out with his son; the Hall went to relatives, who put in tenants, and then to a succession of purchasers. Over the years the interior was much altered and only the fine Elizabethan staircase remains unmistakably from the original building. Nevertheless it had until recently a pleasant exterior, and it was once the home of one of the ablest of the Cheshire gentry, who made a considerable mark in his own day and left plentiful records of his activities behind him.

In his youth he travelled much, visiting not merely the countries usual for an Englishman abroad, such as France and Italy, but Holland, the Spanish Netherlands, Scotland and Ireland. He had been one of the M.P.s for the county in three parliaments before the Civil War broke out and was noted as a strong opponent of Archbishop Laud's high church policy. Like Cromwell, he had no previous military experience; nor had he great wealth or high position. He became commander-in-chief of the parliamentary forces in Cheshire – towards the end of the war, the fourth largest army which Parliament had in the field – because of his zeal, his industry and his organising ability. Unlike Cromwell, he showed no unusual powers as a leader in battle; his principal contribution was the tremendous emphasis which he laid on gaining information about the enemy's movements, at a time when the intelligence service was more often than not haphazard and rudimentary. Raiding cavalry, dragoons, messengers, spies, prisoners of war on both sides, friendly garrisons far and near were all utilised to build up his system, which looked forward to the subsequent establishment of a full-time service.

Wilmslow, the last of the old settlements in the south-east of the commuter belt, was originally the name for the church and the hamlet clustered round it (presumably built on *Wighlem's hlaw,* or mound). The nearby manors were called Pownall and Bollin. Neither manors nor church appear in Domesday Book. The church is all that survives of

medieval times; it stands a little apart and secluded from the hurry and
hubbub of modern Wilmslow, and more islanded with greenery now than
it was in the old days when the village houses huddled close to its eastern
end. Like Cheadle, it is mainly an early sixteenth-century church, but
there has been much more Victorian restoration. It contains a number of
striking effigies of fifteenth- and early sixteenth-century personalities, the
best being a brass of Robert del Booth, who died in 1460, and his wife,
Duce. She brought the manors of Bollin and Dunham to her husband, and
they were the founders of the line of the Booths of Dunham whose
exploits have been mentioned above.

Entirely a farming community until the eighteenth century, Wilmslow
then branched out into a variety of industrial activities. Button moulding
for Macclesfield silk merchants was followed by jersey spinning for
Yorkshire woollen manufacturers. Later the waters of the Bollin and its
tributaries supplied power for small cotton and silk mills. These were
already dead or declining when the first commuters began to arrive. They
came early because there was a station on the original Birmingham-
Manchester line of 1842.

Industry did not die entirely, however, not even the semi-cottage
variety. There was a revival of this when cotton fustian became popular
with workmen because of its hard-wearing quality. The job of cutting the
cloth, so that the cords or ribs stand out, could not be done by machinery
and required a workman moving along the cloth with a knife. It was done
in sheds or even long rooms attached to houses. Besides the fustian
cutters, one water-powered mill survived into modern times. This was the
Quarry Bank Mill a couple of miles outside Wilmslow in the wooded
valley of the Bollin at Styal. Samuel Greg, who founded it in 1784, chose
the site because of the 14-foot fall of water in the river and the local
supply of skilled labour. The wealth his family had already acquired as
manufacturers in Manchester and continued to acquire through mills set
up elsewhere, together with wise technical improvements in the
machinery, enabled the mill to carry on through periods of depression.
Weaving was introduced in 1834, water-driven turbines instead of a
water wheel in 1904. The family retained control throughout, and
acquired a 250-acre estate round the factory. On this were set up the
apprentice houses, for considerable poor house labour was used to begin
with, and later cottages for families of free labour. Farms were bought up

also and their buildings adapted as tenements.

If the appalling hours are overlooked — 5.30 a.m. to 8 p.m., long even for those days — then the Gregs were good employers. They fed their apprentices well and paid careful attention to their health and education. They built a chapel, a shop and a school for the families on the estate. Life at Styal Mill, although hard, seems not to have been brutal or unhappy. Interesting details of it can be read in the recent books on Wilmslow's past by J. H. Hodson. The whole estate was handed over to the National Trust many years ago, and it is hoped to turn the empty mill into a museum illustrating the workings of the machinery and life in the mill village.

FIVE

Stockport and the 'Panhandle'

Even today, when smothered in buildings, the approach to Stockport from the west is dramatic. Past Cheadle Heath the Mersey emerges on the left and the surroundings change from twentieth-century suburban to nineteenth-century industrial. At Brinksway the road runs into a gorge where red sandstone outcrops mingle with factory blocks and terraces of drab little houses. Almost all the houses are unoccupied, but the factories, although they no longer spin nor weave cotton and no smoke belches from their chimneys, are still in use. Soon the road passes under the famous 1840 viaduct, beloved of nineteenth-century artists contrasting engineering feats with industrial squalor, skirts round Stockport's new shopping precinct and fights its way through a welter of more factories, cooling towers and old building sites converted into car parks to the eastern side of the town.

The motorist, eyes fixed on the swirling traffic, will have had just a glimpse on his right-hand side of streets crowding up a steep hill to a church at the top. This is the ancient centre of Stockport, graphically described by William Webb in the early years of the seventeenth century:

'Upon one round hill hath this town of Stockport been built, the summit or top whereof affords the market place and convenient room for the church and for the parsonage which are fair ones . . . the skirt of the hill beautified by many fair buildings, and half about the skirt of it runs the Mersey, with great force or rather fury, under a great stone bridge which divides them from Lancashire.'

14 above *Bosley Cloud, from the Macclesfield canal at Crossley Hall near Congleton.* 15 below *Looking north-east towards the Pennines from Alderley Edge.*

The Mersey's 'fury' has now been tamed and the motorist is unlikely to notice that, in driving through the town, he has crossed and recrossed it. Since 1940 the stretch which ran 'half about the skirt' of the hill has been covered over. On it Stockport's shopping precinct has been built, and even those who may not approve the architecture must admit the boldness of the scheme and the benefits that it confers on the shoppers. Over the centuries Stockport has prided itself on paying special attention to the needs of shoppers. 'It is a great market', said Webb, 'and much frequented by dwellers far remote', and still, every Friday and Saturday, no more than a stone's throw from the sophisticated shopping precinct, the open-air stalls fill the old market place, push up the steps leading to the church and overflow into the narrow streets alongside. It is said that each week close on 130,000 people jostle about the barrows, as their precursors have done ever since 1260 when Edward, Earl of Chester, granted Robert de Stokeport permission for his townspeople to hold a market every Friday. Inevitably the continuity is now threatened by redevelopment schemes for the old centre of the town.

The parish church, which at first glance looks medieval, is now largely an early essay in Gothic Revivalism. Its nave and tower were rebuilt in 1813 by Lewis Wyatt, whose previous work had been in the classical tradition. He left the fourteenth-century chancel with its sedilia and piscina, and the clean lines of his limestone tower and nave replaced crumbling sandstone whose condition had excited the adverse comment of even so convinced a 'gothicist' as John Byng. So his work could be commended, if only he had not encouraged, or allowed, his contractors to throw out all the monuments. Among them went the tombs of the Shaa family before which generations of the boys of Stockport Grammar School had said prayers, as their founder, Sir Edmund Shaa, had enjoined them to do in his will of 1488. Shaa's family were minor gentry from south Cheshire who had settled near Stockport, and Edmund went to London and made his fortune there as a goldsmith. Although not named in the play, he is that complaisant lord mayor in Shakespeare's *Richard III* who gave his blessing to Richard's unscrupulous bid for the throne. That even the warring dynasts themselves accepted that a man of Shaa's type could not be expected to act otherwise (merchants and citizens had only one interest in the struggle: the hope that it might produce firm government and there end) can be seen in Henry Tudor's attitude

16   The west end of Astbury church with its almost detached tower.

towards him. Although Shaa had been cup-bearer at Richard's coronation feast and received a knighthood from him, he was received into Henry's favour and lost neither wealth nor position.

Shaa's will began what is now the oldest school in Cheshire with a record of continuous survival since its foundation. Probably his 'honest priest' who was also to be 'connyng (cunning) in gramer' held the original classes in the church itself. But by the beginning of the seventeenth century the school was housed in the Chestergate. Early in the nineteenth century it moved to a new building on the site of the War Memorial Art Gallery in Greek Street and early in this century to its present building in the Buxton Road. It has had its ups and downs, one of the worst periods being in the nineteenth century when the new Stockport Corporation took over from the Goldsmiths Company as trustees. But the great increase of population in the area and the provision of grants from the Board of Education brought in a period of stability, prosperity and academic and athletic successes. Now with the government decision to end the system of direct grants, this period is drawing to a close and the school, like many others in the north-west whose recent development has been similar, is faced with the agonising decision of whether to accept complete integration into the state system or attempt to go it alone.

Professor Powicke, himself an old boy of the Grammar School, thought Stockport in the time of its foundation, 'with its 14th century church and all the little houses in those steep little streets', must have been one of the most beautiful towns in England. Since the Industrial Revolution crowded the banks of the Mersey and its tributary, the Tin Brook, with mills thirsty for water-power, none have called Stockport beautiful but many have thought it striking. 'The houses ranged upon the hill seem piled upon those in the valley', said one observer early in the nineteenth century, while another, coming after 1821 when the centre of the town was first lighted by gas, wrote:

'The manufactories, rising in tiers above each other, when lighted by the brilliant gaseous vapour of modern discovery, present in the evenings of the winter months a towering illumination of imposing grandeur.'

The last to be impressed (rather to their surprise, one feels) are Pevsner and Hubbard. In their *Cheshire* they concede that Stockport's different levels have been cleverly exploited by recent architects in their construction of shopping precincts and high-rise flats.

The houses 'piled upon' one another had their more unfortunate aspect, however, and so had the driving energy and enterprise of the new mill owners. Despite expansion over the plateau to the south and some belated slum clearance, Stockport had a density rate of 102 persons per acre as late as 1922. A century earlier the conditions on the old town hill, the one immediately south-west of it and under the viaduct and in and out the windings of the Mersey must have been truly appalling. Peter Marsland, Samuel Oldknow and other manufacturers were public-spirited men who gave Stockport good supplies of gas and water long before most other towns had them, and supported the erection of the world-famous undenominational Sunday Schools, as well as churches and other public buildings. Yet, as they toiled themselves without intermission at the businesses which absorbed their interests, they never could understand why their workpeople, although lacking the same compulsive motives, should not do the same. Richard Pilling, the Stockport Chartist leader, said:

'I was twenty years among the handloom weavers and ten years in a factory, and I unhesitatingly say that during the whole course of that time I worked twelve hours a day . . . and the longer and harder I have worked, the poorer and poorer I have become every year until, at last, I am nearly exhausted.'

For over a quarter of a century before Pilling wrote Stockport had been a centre of industrial unrest. There were fierce Luddite (machine-breaking) riots there during the Napoleonic Wars and, in the Radical agitation for manhood suffrage that followed the wars, the Stockport workers were regarded as particularly militant. The weaver poet, Samuel Bamford, hailed them with:

> *Then proudly let our banner wave,*
> *Wi' freedom's emblem o'er it,*
> *And toasted be the Stockport lads,*
> *The lads who bravely bore it.*

This referred to a meeting in 1819 at Sandy Brow, then on the outskirts of the town, when the workpeople drove off with sticks and stones the Cheshire Yeomanry who attempted to take from them their 'Cap of Liberty'. Robert Walmesley, the latest of the many historians of the Peterloo 'Massacre' which took place in St Peter's Fields, Manchester, a few months after the Sandy Brow incident, is convinced that the action of the chief magistrate in calling on the regular cavalry to clear the square was justified by the conduct of the Stockport contingent at the meeting. They had sticks and stones with which they attacked the Yeomanry, and he thinks that the last remark made by the principal speaker, 'Orator' Hunt, before he was arrested, 'if those fellows won't be quiet, put them down and keep them down', referred to them.

Be that as it may, the better times that followed and have, on the whole, been maintained in Stockport, seem to have eroded the town's extremist tendencies. The two great industries of its nineteenth century prosperity, cotton and hat-making, were most fortunately supplemented by others, notably engineering which grew out of what was originally part and parcel of cotton manufactury, the provision of its machinery. When foreign competition hit Stockport's cotton trade after the First World War and finally killed it after the Second, the empty mills were turned to all sorts of new purposes. In them and in new-built factories aircraft engines, atomic reactors, electrical and electronic equipment, man-made fibres, packaged food are all produced. Stockport's good communications position on the southern edge of the industrial belt has helped to make this transition easier here than it has been in many of the old cotton towns further north.

The decline of her other great industry, hat-making, must cause some sorrow, however, for this was an activity peculiar to Stockport and a few neighbouring places. Its origins in the town are obscure but run back at least to the sixteenth century. The big development came in the early nineteenth century with the establishment in the town of the London firm of Christies. By the 1920s there were two other nationally-known firms and many smaller ones as well. Now all are combined in the Associated British Hat Manufacturers Ltd which maintains a precarious existence, although it supplies such markets as remain not only in England but in Europe and even America as well. All this has been caused, not by increasing foreign competition, but through the unexpected abandonment by almost the whole of the northern hemisphere of the time-honoured and not unreasonable habit of wearing a hat!

Medieval remains in Stockport are confined to the chancel of the old church of St Mary's. The Great Underbank has two excellently preserved examples of sixteenth-century timber-framed buildings, both probably town houses for the neighbouring gentry. There are some good Georgian houses, the finest being the Old Rectory in Churchgate, and in Woodbank Park to the east of the town is the columned classical mansion which Thomas Harrison built for Peter Marsland. There is a good run of churches, illustrating both the growth of the town and the changes in architectural fashion. Modest St Peter's shows the beginnings of expansion in 1763; the much larger St Thomas's, with high west tower crowned by a cupola, the greater expansion of the early nineteenth century. Both are classical, although St Thomas's was built ten years later than Wyatt's 'Gothick' rebuilding of the parish church. Finally St George's, out on the Buxton Road, designed by Austin and Paley, is a very late example of the pride and magnificence of high Victorian Gothic. There are plenty of late ninteenth- and early twentieth-century public buildings which are dignified, if unremarkable, and, as before mentioned, the recent designers of flats and shopping centres have taken full advantage of the fact insisted upon both by citizens and writers: that the town is 'built in tiers'. ('And, I should think, conceived in agony', is said to have been the reply of one sardonic visitor who had failed to find any way up from the Underbank to the street above.)

East and north-east of Stockport lies what, until 1974, was that strange prolongation of Cheshire up into the Pennines, the 'Panhandle'. It is bounded by the Etherow, the Goyt and the Tame, whose confluences eventually form the Mersey and, on the far north-east, by Featherbed Moss, the largest of all the Cheshire mosses, whose vast emptiness even the population explosions and industrialisation of the last two centuries have not been able to change. In fact, the upper Etherow Valley below Featherbed Moss, out of which run the passes into Yorkshire at Salters-brook and Bretland Edge, is even more thinly inhabited now than it used to be. At the end of the fifteenth century, Sir Edmund Shaa thought it worthwhile to leave endowments for a chapel and priest at Woodhead as well as for his other foundation of the Grammar School. In 1795 John Aikin said there were three inns and several private houses there and few travellers passed without calling, for if they neglected to get hay for their horses, there would be no other opportunity for a considerable distance. Important modern roads carrying much traffic still run over the old routes and from Woodhead begins the railway tunnel, which when it was first made in 1845 and for many years afterwards was the longest in the world. It was rebuilt in 1954 when the line was electrified. But neither cars nor railway trains nor their passengers need refuelling on journeys as short as these are nowadays, and the inns and their attendant houses have gone.

The rest of the region has been industrialised since the beginning of the nineteenth century. The narrow Tame valley, which used to mark (very inadequately after serious building began) the boundary between Cheshire and Lancashire, is crowded with old mill towns: Hyde, Dukinfield and Stalybridge on the Cheshire side, Ashton-under-Lyne and Mossley on the Lancashire side. Even though cotton is no longer spun and woven and there is the same diversification of industry as in Stockport, and although there are shopping precincts and patches of modern housing, including high-rise flats, this is still predominantly a part of what J. B. Priestley has called the second traditional Britain, the Britain of the original Industrial Revolution. There are huge gloomy mills with tall chimneys and, alongside them, terraces of working-class houses, the older ones solidly constructed of grey gritstone. There are civic buildings and many churches and chapels, mostly ornate nineteenth-century gothic in design, but a few of the older ones, such as Stalybridge's town hall, clinging to the classical traditions of the previous century.

Eastwards along the valley of the Goyt industrialisation has been more sporadic. Indeed, the greenery that begins right inside Stockport with the Vernon and Woodbank Parks brings it home that Stockport, although it has been the largest town in Cheshire since the late eighteenth century, is really quite small. Marple, four miles south-east of Stockport, was industrialised at one bound in the last years of the eighteenth century because it was chosen as the seat of the complex agro-industrial empire which Samuel Oldknow, who had made a fortune as a muslin manufacturer in Stockport, desired to found. Agriculture was by no means driven from Marple, however, and, as the countryside was greener and gentler than in the upper valleys of the Tame and the Etherow, commuters were attracted out from Manchester when the railway link was built in the 1860s.

Christopher Isherwood in his *Kathleen and Frank*, in which he has recreated the lives of his parents through their letters and diaries, shows how at the beginning of this century three stages of Marple's history overlapped in the village. His grandfather, John Bradshaw Isherwood of Marple Hall, was still called 'the Squire' by the shopkeepers because his patronage was valuable to them. But authority had long since passed from the squire to those who employed all the labour in the village, the owners of the mills. And already the old stone houses were being swamped by the red-brick villas of the commuters from Manchester. Since this time the decline of cotton and the rise of the motor car has largely converted Marple into a suburb of Manchester and Stockport.

Nevertheless, even here, Isherwood felt that the dominant impression was of wildness, and this is certainly true of the rest of the region. It is far wetter than any other part of Cheshire – 'never really dries out', according to Isherwood – and in winter is often swept by furious storms of rain or snow. In the nineteenth century annals of Dukinfield and Stalybridge colliery disasters are intermingled with floods, blizzards and even earthquakes!

As might be expected in such a region, the people who were bred in it or came to live in it were 'different'. Once it may well have been one of the last refuges of the Britons from the encroaching Saxons. The *Bretland* of Bretland Edge certainly means 'the land of the Britons'; Tame is a word of British origin and possibly Goyt also. It was a wild and backward region for many centuries after the Saxon takeover – four of its five starveling manors at the time of the Domesday Survey could not raise a full ploughland of arable land between them – but by the seventeenth century there had been some development. There was one sizable village, Mottram-in-Longdendale, whose battlemented medieval church still dominates the now industrialised landscape. There were the estates of many squires with halls, farms and hamlets on them. It was some of these squires who rushed in to defend Manchester from Lord Derby's attack in the first week of the Civil War, when most of their kind elsewhere had not made up their minds on which side to fight or even whether to draw the sword at all.

One of them, Robert Duckenfield, although little more than a boy at the outset of war, rose to command one of Brereton's regiments, and later became the parliamentary governor of Chester. He was an advanced Puritan, who set up a 'gathered congregation' of the faithful under the ministry of a fiery Independent preacher in the chapel of Duckenfield Hall. He rebuked Cromwell at the height of his power, telling him that, although he believed that 'the roots and tree of piety' were still alive in the Lord Protector, 'the leaves thereof through abundance of flatteries seem to be much withered of late'.

The sons of Henry Bradshaw of Marple were also advanced in their views and active in their service. The elder, another Henry, was Duckenfield's second-in-command during the Civil War, and then commanded the regiment himself at the Battle of Worcester, where it distinguished itself. The younger brother, John, was the judge who made history by presiding over the trial of his own sovereign. If you are a Charles the Martyr man, you are unlikely to find any good in that *viper of hell, unawed by divine or human justice*'. John cannot, however, be accused of remaining the catspaw of the military men who undoubtedly pushed him into this position to give an aura of legality to their proceedings. His rebuke to Cromwell for using the army to eject the Rump Government is well known. It is less well known, however, that Cromwell's government, which henceforward regarded Bradshaw as a most dangerous opponent, wanted to remove him from his legal positions in the north-west, but were afraid to do so because he was so well respected there. Among others, the much-persecuted Quakers honoured him for his impartiality and humanity.

By the end of the eighteenth century the little hamlets of Civil War times had swollen into straggling villages of several thousand inhabitants. 'About 25 years ago there was only one house ... now the place looks like a little town', is a typical remark by John Aikin in the north-east Cheshire section of his *Description of the Country from Thirty to Forty Miles around Manchester*. Textile workers, producing wool as well as cotton goods, miners and foundry men (there were mines and iron works in the region then), whether they had been born and bred there or come in from neighbouring places, formed tough communities that were even more radical and militant in the troubled period from 1810 to 1848 than were the Stockport men. 'Go to Stalybridge; there's high pressure', says one of the characters in Disraeli's *Coningsby*. There was strong support for one of the first attempts to organise a big national trade union, and the murder of a Hyde mill owner resulted from the dismissal of an operative for joining this union. In 1842 the Chartist-backed 'Plug Plot', which effectively shut down all the mills in north Cheshire and south Lancashire for a fortnight in an effort to prevent reductions of pay, was organised in a series of meetings held on the moors above Hyde and Stalybridge. Work was stopped in each factory, with or without the support of the factory's own workers, by bands of men who entered the building and extracted the plugs from the boilers. The men from the Panhandle were the first out and the last back in the Plug Plot, although lack of union funds made it extremely difficult in those times to maintain strikes for more than a few days.

The people of Stalybridge and its sister town of Ashton-under-Lyne on the Lancashire side of the Tame also supported that extraordinary character, the Reverend Joseph Rayner Stephens. Stephens, the son of an important member of the Wesleyan Conference in the days after John Wesley's death, himself entered the Wesleyan ministry and came to Ashton and Stalybridge in the 1830s. He was soon in trouble with his father and the Conference for his refusal to isolate religion from the social questions of the day. When they suspended him, he broke away, and for the rest of a long life he and his 'Stephensite' chapels (one in Wellington Street, Ashton, and the other in King Street, Stalybridge) were supported on the voluntary contributions of the members, most of whom were working class. He campaigned unceasingly against what appeared to him to be the two worst evils which affected those around him: the long hours worked in the factories, and the refusal to grant poor relief outside a workhouse which resulted from the Poor Law Amendment Act of 1834. The fame of his oratory, admitted by the judge at his trial at Chester to be unrivalled at the time, led the Chartists to seek his support for their movement to democratise Parliament. He was never very happy under this umbrella, however. To him votes for the poor were only important if they brought with them better living conditions, and he was by no means convinced that they would. He asserted at his trial that he did not believe that 'all power belonged to the people, for it belonged to God', and that he was really a 'church and state' Tory, admiring the ancient nobility and the established church. It was not he who was threatening the constitution but the Whig government, because its new Poor Law took away the rights of the poor.

For a defender of the Establishment, however, his language was sometimes remarkable. To resist the Poor Law, he said, 'it would be law for every man to have his firelock, cutlass, sword, pair of pistols or his pike, and for every woman to have her pair of scissors'. After 18 months imprisonment at Chester for seditious speeches, he quietened down a little, but did not forget his old causes nor his old followers. For 38 more years he continuously supported reductions in working hours in the factories, amelioration of the Poor Law and the strengthening of trade unionism. When he died, thousands attended his funeral service at Dukinfield parish church, and the factory workers of Lancashire and Cheshire erected a monument to his memory. It is a granite obelisk in the pleasant Stamford Park that lies across the old boundary between Ashton and Stalybridge. On it, besides the dedication and some of Stephens' indifferent verses, are a copper medallion bearing his leonine head and an effective sentence from his defence at his trial at Chester: 'The only true foundation of Society is the safety, the security and the happiness of the poor, from whom all other orders of Society arise.'

The industrialisation which was the background to Stephens' life and labours is still there in the Tameside towns. Huge mills rise out of them with terraces of workers' houses alongside. Most of the mills are still in use, although they no longer spin nor weave cotton. There is some continuity in the actual firms also. William Kenyon and Sons began in Dukinfield as rope makers in 1866, and one of their descendant companies in the area today does still make ropes, although now using synthetic as well as natural fibres for them. For an examination of the early beginnings of industry in the region it is necessary to move south to Marple, where the break with the past has been more complete and what is left now is definitely 'industrial archaeology'.

The maker of industrial Marple was Samuel Oldknow, the muslin manufacturer of Stockport. He had made a fortune because the invention of the mule, which could produce yarn that was both strong and fine, enabled delicate muslins, which had hitherto come always from the East, to be made in England. But he was rather an entrepreneur than a real manufacturer at this stage, requisitioning the yarn and doling it out to handloom weavers. Desire to control, quicken and cheapen the production of the yarn led him to set up a water-powered spinning mill in the Hillgate in Stockport and then purchase the Bottoms Hall estate in

Mellor. From 1788 on he built up in the hitherto rural townships of Marple and Mellor a kind of paternal agro-industrial empire of his own. Besides a great mill, employing a work force of over 400, there were warehouses, a dock and a boat-building yard alongside the Peak Forest Canal, which Oldknow played a major part in promoting. He took over farms, planted trees and bred sheep and cattle. Some of these activities did indeed help to find work for the adult male members of the families of his women and child spinners, but one cannot help suspecting that the real motivation was Oldknow's pleasure at starting a multiplicity of enterprises and watching them grow under his hand. It was a dangerous time for such ventures with the great wars against France soaking up capital and damaging trade. Despite his previous fortune Oldknow had twice to be rescued from bankruptcy by the Arkwright family who took over his property at his death. Yet he remained respected and even loved in the Marple-Mellor district. He built roads, a bridge and a chapel for his workpeople, and the surviving evidence is that their lives were far from unendurable. There was certainly none of the resentment against him that there was against the Tameside and Stockport mill owners at the time.

Oldknow's mill has gone, burnt down later in the nineteenth century, but the farm buildings which housed his poor-house apprentices, his bridge, tollhouse, the tower of his church, his lime-kilns and canal warehouse are still there. So, too, is the Peak Forest Canal, with its wonderful series of 16 locks and superb aqueduct (both, without doubt, potent causes of Oldknow's bankruptcy). The aqueduct is accompanied across the wooded valley of the Goyt by the equally splendid railway viaduct of the 1860s, still very much in working order.

Pre-industrial remains in the 'Panhandle' are rarer, more fragmentary and often in incongruous surroundings. Marple Hall survived the Second World War to fall a prey to those twin destroyers, neglect and vandalism. Wybersley Hall, a second seat of the Bradshaws nearer to Disley, is still lived in. It has an early nineteenth-century 'Gothick' front, castellated and crow-stepped, but the rear is stone-built, belonging to an older tradition than Marple Hall, which was of fashionable brick and marked the rise in status of the early seventeenth-century Bradshaws. Wybersley was probably the birthplace of the Judge, who was born while his grandfather was still alive and resident at Marple. Christopher Isherwood, a descendant of the Judge's soldier brother Henry, was certainly born there and, had he wished to do so, could have succeeded as squire of Marple. But he found the atmosphere of an old manor struggling on without power or prestige in an industrial village turning suburban claustrophobic, and put half the world between himself and it.

Portions of Arderne Hall, home of the once important family of the Ardernes, have amazingly survived, although the Hall was deserted and ruinous a hundred years ago. An Elizabethan stone house, it has a tower which looks built for defence and may belong to an earlier period. An even more curious survival has recently been discovered in Stayley Hall which was a second manor of the Booths of Dunham Massey. Its stone exterior encloses an older timber structure. Both Arderne and Stayley Halls are in a dilapidated condition and mixed up with later buildings, some of which are now also ruinous. Much worse is the plight of the last remnant of Duckenfield Hall. It happens to be the most interesting part historically, the chapel where the Colonel's Independent minister and his 'gathered' congregation held their meetings. It was incorporated into a later Congregational Chapel which, surrounded on every side by factories, has now itself become deserted. It is pleasant to be able to record the quite different fate of one old building stranded amidst industrial property. William Kenyon and Sons, referred to previously as one of the oldest firms in the district, have employed an acknowledged expert in such work to restore Newton Hall, a cruck-framed building probably dating back to the fourteenth century. Cruck-framing, which enabled heavier roofing to be employed than the equivalent box-framing, was common in upland areas such as the Panhandle. There *are* surviving examples hidden among the alterations of local farmhouses, but all too few and none open to the visitor, where the materials used and the methods of construction employed can be so clearly seen as at Newton Hall. It is an outstanding example of what can be achieved when the resources of the owners are coupled with an informed desire for conservation. All that is missing is documentary information about those whose built it and lived in it, such as exists for the Ardernes, the Hydes and the Duckenfields whose halls have either disappeared or lie in ruins.

The Panhandle was certainly part of Cheshire when Domesday Survey was made. It is likely that for military reasons it was in it from the very beginning. The seventeenth-century squires seem to have retained some sense of belonging to the rest of the county, but this feeling undoubtedly vanished as far as most of the inhabitants were concerned when the Industrial Revolution came. This obliterated the physical signs of the county boundary. The presence of the Tame between Dukinfield and Stalybridge on the Cheshire side and Ashton on the Lancashire side became hardly perceptible. Higher up the valley from Stalybridge, Mossley was in Lancashire and Saddleworth in Yorkshire. Yet they were like each other; none had any affinity with the Cheshire of the plains, not even with its industrial regions.

So there has been little lamentation in the Panhandle at final severance from Cheshire. The thinly populated Woodhead area has gone into Derbyshire, the rest into Greater Manchester. Not that there is a great deal more enthusiasm for Manchester, convenient as it may be as a shopping and communications centre. It, too, belongs to the softer, more featureless plains. The people of the 'Panhandle' belong only to themselves. 50 years ago folk-speech experts found there dialect words which existed nowhere else. The words have gone now, the spirit remains. At any rate the inhabitants of the Tameside towns should be reasonably satisfied that most of them are now together in their own second-tier authority.

SIX

The
Pennine Border

The Panhandle, thrusting an arm of Cheshire deep into the Pennines, is no more. Yet Cheshire still has a Pennine border, running south and then south-west for nearly 20 miles from Disley to Mow Cop, where the whole range peters out into the North Staffordshire foothills. The land along this border rises to well over 1,000 feet and the names – Shutlings Low, Wincle Minn, Bosley Cloud, Wildboarclough – have a ring of the high hills about them. As Wildboarclough reminds us, this is the edge of a region which was the last refuge in England of the wolf and the boar. The soft red sandstone of the Cheshire plains gives way to harsh millstone grit; all the old farms are built of it. Hedges are replaced by stone walls for boundaries and cattle by sheep. Only the absence of any limestone outcrops and gorges prevents the overwhelming impression that this is Derbyshire and not Cheshire.

Though the hills are bare and forbidding and frequently snow-covered, there are delightful wooded valleys hidden in their folds: the deep and tangled cleft of the Dane on the county's border at Danebridge and, loveliest of all, Wildboarclough, where a little tributary of the Dane flows so placidly for a quarter of a mile or so between green banks that ducks can float on its waters. These spots have many visitors on fine summer weekends, but remain undisturbed for the rest of the year.

On the lower slopes and among the foothills are some signs of the former presence of prehistoric man. Just south of Bosley Cloud lies Cheshire's most ancient relic, the Megalithic tomb known as the Bridestones. Only the main burial chamber remains, divided into two by a broken cross slab which we know once had a 'porthole' in its centre.

The great cairn which covered it has gone and the forecourt is invisible in the surrounding undergrowth. Sufficient is left, however, to identify the Bridestones as a southern outlier of a great group of such cairns centred round the northern end of the Irish Sea. They date from the 3rd millenium B.C. and were the work of Neolithic man. Scattered burials, with or without burial mounds; bronze spearheads and axes, found in the lower sandy ground near Macclesfield and Congleton, reveal that Bronze Age man was in the area. Yet no definite traces of actual habitation have ever been found either for this period or the succeeding centuries of the Iron Age, the Roman occupation or the Saxon invasion. The next relics are the headless shafts of late Saxon crosses standing in remote spots in the hills. The two known as the Bowstones are east of Lyme Park; a single one is at Cleulow Cross four miles south-east of Macclesfield. Three more, removed from their original sites, are in the West Park at Macclesfield. All have round shafts with short square collars above. The two cross-heads covered with interlace that are preserved in the courtyard of Lyme Hall give some idea of the type of heads that these shafts would once have had. They are cruder and more primitive than the earlier Anglo-Norse crosses of the Wirral or the splendid Sandbach crosses, and may not have been connected with actual settlements as these were, but served as landmarks or boundary stones, as well as objects of devotion for the passerby. It is difficult to realise now that they belong to an age which is closer to our own in time than to the age which produced the Bridestones.

Macclesfield, Congleton and a fair scattering of manors in the foothills at the southern end of Cheshire's Pennine border appear in Domesday Book. During the Middle Ages the area developed considerably. Macclesfield became an important royal manor; its burgesses and those of Congleton received a charter. Large parish churches were erected at Gawsworth, Astbury and Prestbury; the Leghs of Lyme and of Adlington, the Fyttons of Gawsworth rose to importance among the county gentry. It was in the eighteenth century, however, during the water-power age, that the eastern border country looked like becoming Cheshire's most important region. Even Wildboarclough had its spinning mill (what is left of it is now the post office), while Congleton and Macclesfield had silk mills and Macclesfield was the centre of Charles Roe's copper smelting empire. For a brief while, before Stockport overtook it, it seemed likely that Macclesfield would become the largest town in Cheshire.

This pace was not maintained. The failure of Roe and other east Cheshire manufacturers and landowners to defeat the Bridgewater and Gower consortium and get parliamentary consent for the Macclesfield-Knutsford canal was the first check. Then local supplies of coal and copper proved insufficient. Really big industrial development became concentrated in south Lancashire and north Staffordshire where coal was plentiful and there was already a big labour force. So, although Macclesfield and Congleton gained distinction as silk towns, their development was limited and the area around them became rural once again as the more isolated water-power mills went out of operation.

The result is a region for the most part delightful to look at and most interesting to visit. A nineteenth-century returning exile wrote of the background:

'As for the country, it is as beautiful as ever; its pastures clothed in as rich a green, its woods with as fragrant and cool a shade as when I first trod them. The old hills, as the blue mists roll from their summits each morning, present the same outline they have borne for ages.'

Against this background are churches and manor houses, some of which are nationally famous either for their architecture or the characters connected with them; old mills, canals and railway viaducts. Industrialisation and urbanisation have never been so overwhelming that they have obliterated what has gone before.

At the northern end of the region, Disley is now select suburbia. Its growth and rebuilding began even before the railway came, partly because of the patronage of the Leghs of Lyme, at whose park gates it stands, and partly because it was the last village along the coaching road to Buxton before, as John Byng put it, 'the country becomes horridly coarse'. One feels that if the *Torrington Diaries* had been known then, instead of being discovered by chance a hundred years later, the Ram's Head would not have been rebuilt, along with the church and the rest of the village, in the nineteenth century. For Byng gave the inn that stood there in his day the most tremendous write-up:

'A neater and more cheerfully situated inn I never saw . . . . The stables

17 above *Hamilton Square, Birkenhead: the Queen Victoria memorial and Town Hall.* 18 below *Early twentieth-century civic 'Baroque' in Stockport Town Hall.*

are excellent, the brown bread and cheese so good, the water so cold, the decanters so clean and the bed rooms so nice that I wished to make a return and pass more time here.'

He did, on his way back from Buxton ('the vilest of all spots') and again commented on the brown bread. (Is this perhaps the first recorded instance of an English preference which continentals find somewhat odd?) He also discovered that parties came out there from Manchester for an evening's jollity, a practice which their modern successors have spread to the whole of Cheshire.

Byng thought Lyme Park 'a dreary waste' and the Hall 'tasteless wasteful grandeur'. Modern experts on such matters and the thousands who have flocked there every year since 1946, when Lord Newton presented it to the National Trust and Stockport corporation undertook its upkeep, would not agree with him. Yet his views do highlight two facts about Lyme whose juxtaposition at first sight seems surprising: that it is set in the most rugged and (until recent times) remote part of Cheshire and yet was – and still is – the grandest house in the county. (It was surpassed in the period from the 1870s to the 1950s by Waterhouse's now vanished Eaton Hall.) The founder of the line of the Leghs of Lyme and builder of the original hunting box on the site of the present Hall was the younger son of one of the Leghs of Adlington, and he gave none too certain a start to the new family by clinging too long to the cause of Richard II in 1399 and getting executed in consequence. Peter Legh, the rebuilder of the house in the early eighteenth century, dabbled dangerously in Jacobitism, being at one time imprisoned in the Tower on suspicion of plotting to assassinate William of Orange and restore James II. These political misadventures, however, did not prevent the Legh wealth from accumulating, and this was the explanation of the grandeur of Lyme. The wealth came mainly from lands just north of Warrington, acquired by marriage. Many of the Leghs of Lyme lie buried in Winwick church, some were M.P.s for the 'rotten' borough of Newton-le-Willows and, when in 1892 W. J. Legh was created a peer, he took the title of Lord Newton.

Inside and out, the Hall is a bewildering jumble of styles as successive owners restored, reshaped and added. In the 1720s the Italian architect, Giacomo Leoni, an expert on the work of the famous Renaissance

19 Saxon cross shafts at Sandbach; the Nativity and the Crucifixion are portrayed on the nearer.

architect Palladio, reshaped the Elizabethan house which had already received a number of alterations. He added wings to the north front but left its complicated Elizabethan porch of four tiers. He completely rebuilt the south front with 15 bays adorned with giant pilasters and, in the middle, a giant portico. The greater part of the interior remains Elizabethan, even the long gallery surviving, but there are additions and alterations made not only by Leoni but by architects in Victorian, Edwardian and modern times. There are Elizabethan and Jacobean fireplaces with elaborate overmantels in stone, plaster and wood, plaster ceilings of three different centuries, a set of pearwood carvings Gibbonesque in style and execution if not by Grinling Gibbons himself, a staircase in the grand Leoni manner. Yet this jumble is held together by its pervading richness and the sense of continuity given by the arms and portraits of the Leghs, which are everywhere. Outside, set in the great park and against the background of the hills, the Hall looks compact and unified.

A few miles south-west of Lyme, really just out of the foot-hills of the true Pennine border region, is Adlington Hall, home of another branch of the Leghs. Adlington is less grand than Lyme, but just as jumbled and just as full of interest. Originally it was all timber-framed. The great hall is still open to its roof, the finest hammerbeam roof in Cheshire. At its east end are two huge oak supports, said to date from the hunting lodge that preceded the Hall, at its east end a panelled canopy with heraldic designs. There was much patching in brick after the considerable damage caused during the Civil War. Then, in mid-eighteenth century, there was a vast rebuilding by Thomas Legh, for which possibly he was his own architect. He used bricks which were burnt in a kiln situated in the park, but his south front has an impressive stone portico with a pediment and four great pillars. The greater part of his west wing, which included a ballroom, has been pulled down to reduce maintenance costs, for Adlington, unlike Lyme or Tatton, is still occupied by its founding family. The Leghs of Adlington were particularly distinguished during the Civil War for active loyalty to their sovereign. The head of the house, Thomas Legh, his brother and his five sons, all held commissions from the king, and the Hall was twice besieged. The damage to it was considerable, for timber mansions hardly make the best of fortresses, and the fines imposed on the family were heavy.

Back in the hills are the tiny hamlet of Pott Shrigley and the little industrial town of Bollington. In their different ways both are remarkable. Pott Shrigley's late medieval church contained at the end of the fifteenth century a *lending library*! Geoffrey Downes, brother of the local squire, was a Fellow of Queens' College, Cambridge, and left a collection of religious books, printed and in manuscript, in the chantry that he had just founded in the church. Any gentleman who wished could borrow any of them for thirteen weeks, 'soe that he Leave sufficient pledge to keep them safe and bring them again'. Bollington, which does not stand on the river Bollin but on its tributary the Dean (the place-name experts suggest that this once shared the name of the greater stream), is an interesting survival. It began to develop about the same time as Marple but without a great father-figure like Oldknow. Whatever it had been to begin with, in the nineteenth century it became predominantly a cotton town. Canal and railway communication came to it late and it did not expand greatly. The main line from Manchester through Macclesfield to London by-passed it and deposited the commuters at Prestbury three miles away to the west. So, unlike Marple, it has remained mainly working class and industrial. Its two great mills, the Clarence and the Adelphi, although these are now used for other purposes, and its stone housing still dominate the town.

Prestbury, again really out of the foothills, is said to be the 'swell-belt's' most select commuter suburb today. Before the twentieth century it was famous only for its parish church and the charming little village which had grown up around it. Prestbury parish was so vast that at one time it included Macclesfield and over thirty other townships. The very name means 'priest's manor' and although, strangely enough, it does not appear in Domesday Book, there is ample evidence of the early establishment of Christian worship there. In the churchyard are fragments of a Saxon cross and the front, with doorway and tympanum, of a Norman chapel. The church itself and its furnishings contain work of every century from the thirteenth to the nineteenth and are almost a history of the English parish church in themselves. Despite the recent development, some care has been taken to preserve the village street, whose greatest treasure is the little two-storeyed timber-framed house opposite the entrance to the churchyard.

Macclesfield has had many claims to distinction in its long history. In the Middle Ages it was a kind of capital of eastern Cheshire. The administration of the Hundred of Macclesfield, one of the seven areas into which the county was divided, was centred there. In addition, the earl's Forest of Macclesfield, which stretched east of the town as far as the county border, north as far as Marple and south as far as Bosley, held its courts there. Macclesfield was an important manor of both the Norman and the royal earls, breeding horses, among them the great *destriers* for the armoured knights, and fattening cattle for the larders at Chester and Westminster. Its importance soon enabled its inhabitants to win privileges from their lords. Their first charter came from Earl Ranulf III about 1220, the next (still extant) from the future Edward I in 1261. By the end of the Middle Ages important people thought it worth while to acquire property and influence in Macclesfield. The castellated mansion which once stood in the Backwallgate was put up by John de Macclesfield, Keeper of the Wardrobe to Richard II. Later the Buckingham family acquired this, and that Duke of Buckingham who helped Richard III to the throne and was later executed for turning against him, was often in the town and noted for his lavish entertainment. The rising west Cheshire family of the Savages, who helped Henry Tudor to supplant Richard, obtained the lease of the corn mills and the royal park.

The effigies and tombs of these Savages in the chantry chapel put up by Thomas Savage, Archbishop of York, are the only surviving relics of Macclesfield's medieval period. Even the remainder of the parish church to which the chapel is attached is Victorian. The complete plate armour of the effigies of Sir John Savage, who commanded a wing of Henry Tudor's army at Bosworth, his father and his son, contrast strikingly with the elaborate but largely ornamental armour of an Elizabethan Sir John Savage and the vast wig and flowing robes of Earl Rivers, one of the last of the line, who died in 1694. For the rest, only the names of a few of the streets – Chestergate, Jordangate, Backwallgate – their narrowness and the way they crowd up to the church on the summit of the old town hill, suggest the Middle Ages.

After a period of comparative obscurity in Elizabethan and Stuart times, Macclesfield again became prosperous and important in the eighteenth century. This was despite a traumatic experience in 1745, when the town was occupied for five days by Bonnie Prince Charlie's

Highland clansmen. The inhabitants, whose superiors were all solidly Whig, stared in astonishment and alarm at this incursion from another world. They complied with the demands of the Jacobites – money, provisions and an official welcome – but grudgingly, and gave them no recruits. In view of this they were lucky that the Highland army was under good discipline, and did no harm to their persons and nothing like as much as had been feared to their property.

The '45 was soon no more than an almost unbelievable memory, and the town turned back to developing its coal, its copper and its silk manufactury. Making buttons of silk on a wood base had been widespread in cottages in and around Macclesfield for some time, the silk being brought up from London. But big developments were now in the air. Huguenot refugees had brought to south-eastern England the art of silk 'throwing' (the spinning of fine silk thread). The secret of water-powered silk-throwing machinery had been filched from Italy and used to set up a silk mill at Derby. The patent for this had expired and three years before the Jacobites came Charles Roe, a button merchant, established the first silk mill in Macclesfield. In the very year of the '45 John Brocklehurst, a chapman (travelling salesman), joined with two other button merchants to set up as silk manufacturers. Roe soon pulled out of silk to put his capital into copper smelting, but the Brocklehurst enterprise developed into a family concern which set up silk-throwing mills and after two generations went into weaving as well. In the nineteenth century J. & T. Brocklehurst had the largest silk weaving mill in the country and won prizes at the Great Exhibition of 1851. As Brocklehurst-Whiston Amalgamated Ltd the firm has continued into modern times.

Silk manufacturing in Macclesfield was not all by great firms like the Brocklehursts, however. As late as 1927 H. V. Morton was staggered to see a notice in a Macclesfield window saying: 'WANTED Six thred figured hand-loom weavers'. Investigating, he found sixty men in a long shed weaving on hand-looms the material from which very expensive ties, sold in exclusive London shops, would be made up. One of the men told him that the satisfaction of creating something and not just minding a machine more than compensated for the heaviness of the work. The hand-looms are silent now, but they lasted almost as long as the manufacture of silk itself in Macclesfield.

The manufacture of silk in Britain has always been a chancy business. In addition to the normal drawbacks of making a luxury article whose sale may contract in difficult times or through changes in fashion, inability to produce the raw material has always put Britain in a weak position against competitors such as France and Japan who can and do produce it. So the manufacture of man-made fibres and a variety of other industries paralleled in many other Cheshire towns have taken over from silk in Macclesfield. Doubtless the worker has better pay and better conditions under Geigy or I.C.I. or most of the other concerns now tidily established on the industrial estate at Hurdsfield. Only, as Macclesfield-born author Graham Turner has said, there cannot be any of the old pride in owning to these new occupations and explaining to the stranger that 'Macclesfield *used* to be a great silk-making town'.

Charles Roe, when he pulled out of silk manufacturing, entered on a career foreshadowing that of the American tycoons of the next century. In 1762, using copper from the old mines at Alderley, he set up smelting works on the common east of the town. The next year he began yet more works at a place on the Dane north of Congleton where there was a splendid head of water. As no village was there already, he had to build one, and he called it Havannah to commemorate the capture of this port by the British navy in the same year. Within a few more years he had begun copper and brass rolling mills at Havannah and at Bosley.

The enterprise soon began to move outwards. Brass-making needed calamine and Roe took leases on a mine at Mold. Rightly thinking the supplies of copper at Alderley uncertain, he took leases on mines in the Lake District and Anglesey. When his scheme for a canal from Macclesfield to the Weaver Navigation foundered, he set up a new smelting works near Liverpool. After Roe's death in 1781 the Macclesfield Copper Company leased mines in the Wicklow mountains and set up yet more smelting works in South Wales. By this time, with their poor communication and lack of raw materials, the works in east Cheshire had become unprofitable and an embarrassment. Those on Macclesfield common were closed down in 1801, those at Havannah and Bosley went over to silk soon after. The business was now out of the hands of the Roe family and lost all connection with the county.

There are some relics of this early meteor of Cheshire big business. The factories and cottages of Havannah are of later date, but Roe's beautiful weir is still there. In Macclesfield itself his chief surviving monument is Christ Church, built largely at his expense in 1773 and only the second church to be erected in the town. It is hardly a beautiful church; its tower appears too slim for the squat bulk of the nave and aisles, and the proportions seem to waver between the graceful and the monumental and achieve neither. But inside is a tablet to Roe put up shortly after his death. It has on it a portrait medallion and reliefs of Roe's three creations in Macclesfield: the church itself, the Park Green Silk Mills and the copper works on the common. This portrait was used later for the copper halfpennies issued by the company under government licence. Byng bought 6d worth of them in 1790, declaring that they were 'of much better make and value than the government can afford'.

Relics of these early days of Macclesfield's industrial development are fast vanishing, but one very large mill, known as the Card Factory, still remains on the Chester Road and two more near Park Green. Mill Street itself is now entirely given over to shops. In the Market Place is the fine classical Town Hall of 1823 and near it the Macclesfield Arms Hotel of the same period. Further down the Jordangate are the early Georgian Jordangate House, where some of the Brocklehurst family once lived, and Cumberland House, where the Duke stayed while following up the Jacobite retreat. Now that its Stockport counterpart has gone, the large Sunday School of 1813 in Roe Street is the surviving relic of that, for a time, successful attempt to give an elementary education that was non-sectarian.

Four miles south-east of Macclesfield in a most beautiful setting of avenues of trees and ornamental pools lies Gawsworth. It is, in origin, a church, a manor house and a rectory; only circumstances duplicated the last two buildings. Such village as there was was nearly a mile away at Warren, where there is now much commuter development. Of Gawsworth itself, the beauty of its buildings and the tangled lives of those who lived in them, and disputed and fought over them, only a glimpse can be given here. A whole book has been written about them and to this, *The Manor of Gawsworth* by Raymond Richards, the reader is referred. The author could hardly be better qualified. He has lived in the Old Rectory, now owns the Old Hall, is lord of the manor and patron of the church.

Church, Old Hall and Old Rectory were all first built in the fifteenth century. The Rectory and the Hall are both timber-framed and the Rectory retains its medieval great hall with open, steeply pitched roof. The Hall, like Bramall, Moreton and Speke in Lancashire, had its great hall divided up and a multitude of additional 'chambers' added during Tudor times. Its eventual shape was quadrangular, but the decay that followed on the Civil War and disputes as to ownership caused a later owner to pull down one and a half sides lest they 'fall on his head'.

The church is constructed of a mixture of grey gritstone from the Cheshire hills and red sandstone from its plain, thus demonstrating that Gawsworth stands on the dividing line between the two strata. It has a lovely slender tower, a wide aisleless nave with great Perpendicular windows and a richly carved camber-beam roof. The exuberance of the medieval mason is well displayed in the gargoyles and the heads on the hood-moulds.

In the chancel crowding round the altar are the tombs of the Fyttons. In the seventeenth century, when some of the tombs had canopies, they must have emphasised even more strongly how much the lord of the manor dominated the parish church. The Fyttons became nationally important, as did many of the Cheshire squirearchy in Elizabethan and Jacobean times, through the services they rendered and the lands they acquired in Ireland. In fact the tomb of the greatest of them, Sir Edward Fytton who was Treasurer for Ireland and Lord President of Connaught in Elizabeth's reign, does not lie here but in St Patrick's Cathedral, Dublin. The tomb of the last of the direct line of the Fyttons, another Sir Edward, is in Gawsworth and with it a long inscription extolling him as a paragon of all the virtues in peace and war. Alas, recent research in the archives of his first wife's family, the Trevors, has revealed that he was perpetually borrowing money, minded 'nothing but a voluptuous life and neglects his estate wholly', and sometimes made himself ill 'through extremity of drinking'. His better side came to the front when war broke out. While others were wavering, he enthusiastically raised a regiment from the local youth, and led it through the campaign which included the battle of Edge Hill and the storming of Bristol. He died in 1643, not of wounds as is sometimes said, but probably of consumption.

He was childless and, after the death of his second wife, a tremendous dispute over the succession to the Gawsworth estates arose between his brother-in-law, the royalist general Sir Charles Gerard, and his cousin,

Alexander Fytton. It got mixed up with high politics, for Alexander became a supporter of the right of James, Duke of York, to succeed to the throne, and Gerard, a Whig opponent of this, despite his strongly royalist past and the reward of the Earldom of Macclesfield from Charles II. Gerard's politics brought about a notable scene on the piece of level ground near the Hall which is always supposed to have been a medieval tilting ground. When Monmouth visited Cheshire in 1682, he was not only entertained by a banquet in the Hall and hunting in the park, but by a game called *Prison Bars* performed on the tilting ground. This was a team game very popular in Cheshire at the time and consisted of running, touching and capturing opponents in a confined area. It would have been appreciated by Monmouth, himself a keen sportsman, but this and other activities during the Duke's visit to Cheshire put the earl of Macclesfield under grave suspicion. When James came to the throne and Monmouth's desperate rising failed, he had to flee the country. He came back in triumph with William of Orange, however, and occupied Gawsworth again. His rival, Alexander, got no more than the empty title of Baron Fytton of Gawsworth from the exiled James II.

This was not the end of sensational disputes over Gawsworth. The earl of Macclesfield's grandson died childless and a new succession dispute arose between the husbands of the grandson's two nieces, Lord Mohun and the Duke of Hamilton. They were men of rank and fashion at the court of Queen Anne, and in 1712 they killed each other in a duel fought in Hyde Park which had arisen out of a quarrel over the estate. This caused a sensation in society at the time, the queen herself being particularly distressed about it, but it ended Gawsworth's appearance on the national scene. The descendants of the Duke's widow by another husband finally inherited without further dispute, but they rarely resided in or even visited their new acquisition.

Mohun, in his brief tenure of Gawsworth, added two buildings, a new hall and – surprisingly for a noted rake and duellist – a school for the parish. The New Hall, which he did not live to finish, remained exceedingly plain, its only decorative feature being a modern main door. It is now a home for the elderly. The school was plain also and very small, so that in the nineteenth century the children were moved to a larger school in Warren. The old school, with some interesting adornments brought from elsewhere, is now the New Rectory.

The lovely country between Macclesfield and Congleton contains two outstanding monuments of nineteenth-century engineering. The Macclesfield Canal, joining the Peak Forest Canal at Marple to the Trent and Mersey at Harding's Wood, was not completed until 1831. By this time the Railway Age was under way and so it was never a great commercial success. Nevertheless, designed by Telford, it is a beautiful piece of engineering. Particularly interesting spots to visit along it are the two 'roving' bridges south of Congleton, designed to enable horses to cross over the canal, when the tow-path changed sides, without the tow-rope being unhitched; and the seven locks near Bosley. These were built to bring together the northern and southern sections of the canal, each of which followed a different contour line and was lockless.

Schemes for railway lines to and from Macclesfield encountered as much opposition from already established rivals as had the canal schemes. The Grand Junction Railway Company took the place of the Duke of Bridgewater. One hopeful new venture got as far as persuading a mayor of Congleton to lay a foundation stone for its viaduct across the Dane before it was strangled. Eventually the more powerfully backed North Staffordshire Railway did build a viaduct (in a different place). It is a massive affair of 20 arches in brick and stone. Designed by Robert Stephenson, it was constructed by Thomas Brassey, perhaps the greatest railway contractor of all time. He built railways all over the world but, although born and brought up in Cheshire, there is little of his work in the county. This viaduct, the Ethelfleda bridge between Runcorn and Widnes, and Chester General Station are the only outstanding examples.

Congleton has similarities to Macclesfield. It climbs around and up one of the foothills of the Pennines. It was a manor at the time of the Domesday Survey, obtained its first charter in the thirteenth century and developed a strong municipal corporation which lasted until 1974. Its excellent water-power facilities led to cotton and silk mills being established there and both industries survived into the twentieth century.

It has always been smaller than Macclesfield and never hit the national headlines. No grandees built palaces in it or marched from it to decide the nation's destiny. John Bradshaw spent some years in it as a lawyer and became its mayor, but he left before he attained national eminence. Although at one period it produced more thrown silk than Macclesfield, it never became known as *the* silk town. It would be a great mistake, though, to regard it simply as a smaller Macclesfield. It is a town of great individuality and character and immensely proud of its long history of municipal government. In 1972 it staged a celebration to mark the 700th anniversary of its first charter, which in length and variety could not have been outdone by a town fifty times its size. It lasted a whole year and included an official visit by the Queen and the publication of a well-documented and authoritative history of the town. It is good that the planners have made it the centre of one of the new county districts but, even without this, its long tradition, its situation (surrounded by country and away from any other urban development) and the cheerful and independent nature of its inhabitants make it unlikely that it would have lost its identity.

Nothing whatsoever remains of medieval Congleton, and from Tudor and Stuart times there are only two inns and one or two smaller buildings in High Street and West Street. In Mill Green two storeys remain of Congleton's first silk mill. In 1752 the example of Stockport and Macclesfield and the desire to keep the town's poor off the rates led the corporation to lease land to John Clayton, silk spinner of Stockport, and Nathaniel Pattison, silk merchant of London. They brought in Brindley, already famous locally as a genius at hydraulics although not yet as a canal engineer, to design their machinery. Subsequent growth in prosperity and population is shown by the building in 1740 of St Peter's Church to replace the chapel of ease in Chapel Street, and by the pleasant early nineteenth-century houses round about it with their ironwork porches and balconies.

The Town Hall, although it is difficult to view it satisfactorily because of the narrowness of the High Street in which it stands, is a worthy monument to Congleton's nineteenth-century enterprise and development. It was designed in the High Victorian Gothic manner by the well-known architect E. W. Godwin. It has a castellated and machicolated tower and statues on its façade to Queen Victoria, Henry de Lacy, who granted the town's first charter, and Edward I, who was the first monarch to visit it. This type of architecture was only just beginning to be accepted in the provinces. At the time Chester was putting up a town hall in similar style, but no other Cheshire town followed suit for another 20 years.

Because it is unremarkable outside and in a quiet backwater, St Peter's, Congleton, tends to be overlooked. But its interior reveals the eighteenth-century pattern of church design, a flat, shallow chancel and a wide nave with galleries so that all the congregation could see and hear every part of the service. There are not many such churches in Cheshire and no other has a relic such as Congleton possesses, the large pulpit still standing in the centre of the nave. It recalls the era when even the Church of England regarded the sermon as the core of the service. It is amazing that it has survived. Has the Oxford Movement never come in strength to Congleton?

A mile south of Congleton is Astbury, once the parish church for the town and the best known of all Cheshire parish churches outside the county. It deserves its reputation. Although just off the main road to the Potteries, it has about it only a handful of charming cottages. There are fragments of an earlier church, but the greater part of the present building was put up between 1350 and 1540. The tall double-storeyed west porch and the almost detached west tower with its delicate spire are the features which strike the visitor most as he comes in from the road. The long series of aisle windows – there is no break between nave and chancel – have the flowing tracery of the fourteenth century, but the clerestory windows above them and the huge east window have the straight lines of Perpendicular tracery, thus revealing that the nave was raised after the aisles had been built. The interior is light and spacious, and contains the finest camber-beam roof and the finest rood screen in a county noted for both timber roofs and screens. The screen has lierne vaulting and its carving of fruit, flowers and foliage is so free and uninhibited that the influence of Celtic craftsmen from the border to the south is suspected. The roof has great pendants hanging from it and is rich with interlace on the beams and shields, monograms and crows' feet on the bosses. In addition there are many interesting wooden furnishings, dating mostly from the seventeenth century: box pews, communion rail, pulpit, an eagle lectern and a great font cover.

Three miles further south is an even more widely known Cheshire building, Little or Old Moreton Hall. Endlessly reproduced on cards and calendars it has become *the* example of an 'olde worlde' timber English mansion. At first sight it is almost unbelievable. I remember once taking a party of students to see it, and the first one to tumble out of the coach and get a full view exclaimed, 'But it's a fake. It *must* be.'

What excites disbelief is the ubiquity of the black and white patterns –

for brick appears only in the great chimneys — and the crazy tilt of the third storey long gallery above the gatehouse. Yet the black and white is throughout genuine, in that it results from the timber framing and is not a façade, while an expert on the Hall has said, 'Its slanting walls and undulating roofs give a romantic but erroneous impression of decay.' Structurally it is still very sound.

Moreton gains nothing by associations, romantic or otherwise, for none are known. The Moreton family lived in it from the late Middle Ages until just after the Civil War, and then put tenants into it until descendants handed it over to the National Trust in 1937. They made no great mark in local affairs, let alone national ones. As a result, not only are there no rooms legitimately associated with Mary, Queen of Scots, Charles I, James II or Monmouth, but no one has ever been tempted to suggest such associations.

Furnishings are slight in Moreton also, so interest centres almost entirely on the structure of the house itself. As there is no documentary evidence as to its erection and only one date on the building itself, the experts have to go on refinements such as window mouldings, and frequently get themselves into a great tangle as to the order in which different parts were put up. The general pattern is clear enough, however. The great hall on the northern side was built first, probably towards the end of the fifteenth century, and was open to the roof and with kitchen, buttery and pantry at its west end and a solar above them. In the sixteenth century, with the growing emphasis on privacy, the hall was given a ceiling and rooms put above it, a parlour was added at its eastern end and a withdrawing room beginning an eastern range. Hall and withdrawing room were lighted by bay windows into the courtyard (one of these has the date 1559 on it). A multiplicity of chambers then continued down the eastern range culminating in a private chapel, but it is possible that before this range was completed a leap forward was taken and the gatehouse to the south begun. It has been suggested that the dangerous-looking overhanging and tilting of the long gallery that crowns it was due to this being an afterthought added after the construction of the gatehouse had been planned and begun. The western range was never carried far enough to complete the quadrangle. The piecemeal nature of Tudor building is admirably revealed at Moreton because there was no eighteenth-century reconstruction, as at Lyme and Adlington, to impose an illusion of symmetry upon the whole.

Above the Hall is an outcrop of rocks known as Mow Cop which is crowned by a folly. This, consisting of a 'ruined' tower and some walling, was placed there in mid-eighteenth century by Randle Wilbraham of Rode to enhance the view from the new hall which he had built below. At the beginning of the nineteenth century the spot was celebrated for something less aristocratic and playful than a folly. The Primitive Methodists, who drew much of their strength from the industrial areas of the Potteries and east Cheshire, held there the great revivalist meetings which led to their break away from the main body of the Methodists.

The sprawling buildings running up on the far side of Mow Cop are in Staffordshire and the outskirts of the Potteries. Elsewhere, notably at Scholar Green and Alsager, these outskirts have flowed across the border into Cheshire. In the carve-up of the county contained in the original Redcliffe-Maud proposals, this was the only slice of the old Cheshire not allotted to Manchester or Liverpool. Instead it was to be put under Stoke. Although this has not come about, the communications and services of this area do derive mainly from the Potteries.

SEVEN

Central Cheshire: The Plain

The Cheshire plain has been compared to a bowl or basin, or even a hammock slung between the Pennines and the Flintshire hills. A not very comfortable hammock and a not very smooth bowl, however, because not only are there isolated outcrops, like Alderley Edge and Beeston, and many undulations in it, but it is divided by a considerable ridge. This Central Ridge (see Chapter Nine) runs north and south and rises in places to 700 feet. West of it there is a narrow irregular plain fanning out from the valleys of the Dee and the Gowy into the Wirral and the Ince and Frodsham marshes. East of it the plain is much larger and unbroken. It slopes gently from the north and east into the valleys of the Weaver, the Dane and the Wheelock, all of them broad and shallow and, to the speeding motorist, hardly noticeable.

The whole of this eastern plain is underlain by the variety of sandstone rock known as the Keuper Marl, and from the deposits in these rocks has sprung Cheshire's oldest industry – salt making. But salt making and its modern chemical successor (see Chapter Eight) have always been concentrated in a narrow strip lying in the valleys of the Weaver, the Dane and the Wheelock. The wanderer over the other parts of the plain will often be out of sight of their manifestations altogether and only conscious of them when they are very close at hand.

Most of the plain is still rural. There is a certain amount of light industry scattered about and, under the old administrative system, two urban district areas, Knutsford and Sandbach. Both are old market towns; the former has a large and well-established commuter element, the latter a small but increasing one. A number of very important roads, including the M6 and the A556 from Manchester to Chester, cross the plain. Although the amount and nature of traffic on them would bewilder any of its inhabitants brought up prior to the twentieth century, it is no new thing for them to live alongside a great road system. Modern research has established three stretches of roadway hereabouts as being certainly Roman in origin with two more a possibility. In the early seventeenth century, according to Webb, Cranage on the outskirts of Holmes Chapel was a famous 'baiting' place, i.e. halt for rest, refreshment and change of horses. There the road from London and the Midlands divided into the roads to the north via Warrington and via Manchester. 'Drunken Barnaby' (in his sober moments Richard Braithwaite, Westmorland squire, Cambridge graduate and classical scholar) confirms this in his rhymed pub-crawl from his home to London via the Warrington route.

> *Thence to the Cock at Budworth where I*
> *Drank strong ale as brown as berry.*

and

> *To Holmes Chappell forthwith set I;*
> *Maid and hostess both were pretty;*
> *But to drink took I affection,*
> *I forgot soon their complexion.*

Away from the main roads is a maze of by-roads, most of which would have been already there in Drunken Barnaby's day. Their surfaces nowadays are very creditable and they are wonderfully peaceful. Although their winding and undulating nature makes too close an attention to the view unwise for the car driver, he can gain a strong enough impression of the countryside. Though there is a certain amount of arable farming in Cheshire and it is the southern end of the county that has been called 'the high temple of dairy farming', yet in the Central Plain too the overwhelming impression is of pasture and meadow land. And, although paddock and zero grazing have come to Cheshire, there are still plenty of herds on view, the Friesian variety dominating more and more after the 1967-8 foot-and-mouth epidemic caused Canadian and continental strains to be brought in to replace the old stock. In quiet corners everywhere are old farms and cottages containing sections in timber and plaster or in brick that date back to the late seventeenth and early eighteenth centuries and have been embedded in later improvements. There are old mills, too, some with only the mill houses left, some with old machinery and mill ponds as well, a handful still working. Of the last the best known and most convenient to visit is the Nether Alderley mill on the opposite side of the A34 from the parish church. It now belongs to the National Trust. Dating from as far back as the fifteenth century, it is a stone building roofed with Kerridge slabs that sweep down almost to ground level. Its two overshot wheels are worked from a pool on higher ground behind the mill and invisible. This was once the moat of the old Alderley Hall which was burnt down in 1779.

Even before it became inseparably linked with Mrs Gaskell's *Cranford*, Knutsford had the reputation of being a pleasant town. Webb said it was 'a fine market and pleasantly situated'; Byng that it was 'a clean, well-built, well-placed town'. It once had a large water-powered silk mill, and Byng attributed its prosperity (as he did a great deal else in the neighbourhood) to the cotton trade. But Aikin more correctly diagnosed that 'it has never been a place of much trade'. Despite some recent light industry this still remains true today. It is the town's pleasant situation and good communications that attract inhabitants.

Mrs Gaskell brought a railway to her Cranford 20 years before the real one arrived in Knutsford. When it did come in 1862, 'villas' soon began to spring up; today there are considerable commuter suburbs. But Knutsford was a place of importance in the county long before Mrs Gaskell or the railway appeared in it. In 1623 Webb spoke of its market as 'greatly frequented' and the town as 'extraordinarily well traded'. In 1795 Aikin said it was the principal town of Bucklow Hundred and a few years later George Ormerod in his great *History of the County Palatine of Chester* called it 'the metropolis of the Eastern Hundreds'. These statements seem to suggest that Knutsford was once a kind of rival to Chester's greatness. It was never that, but it is true that prior to the railway age it was the only convenient centre for activities in the north of the county.

Webb thought its importance stemmed from the influential gentry whose estates were around the town. Certainly within a ten-mile radius of the town there was a group of gentry which for status, ancient lineage and landed wealth could compare with any in the county. The group included the Leghs of Norbury Booths, the Leicesters of Tabley and the Leicesters of Toft, the Egertons of Tatton, the Booths of Dunham and the Warburtons of Arley.

The Civil War split this group apart and even divided one of its individual families. The heir of Daniel of Over Tabley and one of his brothers died fighting for King Charles; two of the other sons fought for the Parliament, one of them rising to be an important officer of the New Model Army. John Legh of Norbury Booths, lord of the manor of Over Knutsford, was a zealous officer of Brereton's. Presumably most of the Knutsford men who enlisted were in his regiment and therefore fought for Parliament. Yet he never attempted to fortify the town and there was no fighting in or near it. Passing armies of both sides bivouacked on Knutsford Heath, one of the few remaining large open spaces in a county by this time heavily enclosed. But these armies were usually so large or so formidable (Prince Rupert commanded one of them) that there was no opposition. The one exception was right at the end of the struggle in 1651 when the Heath was very nearly the site of a major battle. Despite their commander's absence, Cromwell's subordinates, Generals Lambert and Harrison, were willing to fight the Scots army which young Charles II was leading into England. Charles was eager for battle too, but the Scots commanders were nervous of what the New Model cavalry might do on the open ground of Knutsford Heath. So they persuaded Charles to march on, to the destruction of all his hopes at the Battle of Worcester a few weeks later.

The subsequent history of Knutsford Heath has been more peaceful and sportive. We do not know when horse races were first held on it, but by the end of the eighteenth century they were well established. Aikin said they were 'inferior to few in the kingdom for the display of fashionable company', but the lofty Byng was contemptuous of both course and company. Today the chief event on the Heath is the Royal May Day Festival with its fair and carnival procession culminating in the crowning of the May Queen. The Knutsford May Day is distinguished from the myriad revivals of this ancient pagan festival all over the country by a custom which seems to be peculiar to the town itself. Certain streets are swept and the pavements covered with sand, and elaborate patterns then made with strips of white sand among the brown. This custom has not always been associated with the May Day Festival. In the eighteenth and early nineteenth century it was used particularly to celebrate weddings and there is a yet earlier recorded instance of it being employed for a special occasion. In 1682 the streets were strewn with sand and flowers to welcome the Protestant 'hero,' the Duke of Monmouth. It is probable that 'sanding' in Knutsford has been adapted to fit various purposes and stretches back through the centuries to unrecorded times.

There is little doubt that Knutsford was originally 'Knut's Ford', but who was Knut and where was the ford? Knutsfordians naturally like to think that their founder was the famous ruler of England, Denmark and Norway but, although this is not impossible, it is unprovable. The Norse presence in Cheshire was considerable, and there may have been more than one Knut who was locally important in his day although forgotten now. As to the ford, the little brook that runs parallel to King Street and empties itself into Tatton Mere is so insignificant that it is difficult to imagine the sea-rovers bothering to find a ford across it, let alone commemorating the finding in a name. There is another possibility, however: that the first Knutsford may have lain nearer the larger stream of the Birkin. There is clear evidence that a *new* town of Knutsford was founded somewhere about the fourteenth century, and the Middle Ages left quite a bewildering multiplication of places either bearing the name Knutsford or connected with it: Nether Knutsford, Over Knutsford, Cross Town, Knutsford Booths. Recent rapid expansion has still not covered with bricks and mortar all the land embraced by these names. Fortunately there has been a strong revival recently of interest in Knutsford in its archaeology and history. Good work has been done in excavating an early manor house of the Leghs of Knutsford and Norbury Booths and it is hoped that a re-appraisal and re-writing of the early history of the town may result also. So far knowledge of this has relied on the genealogical studies of Ormerod and the entertaining, but vague and discursive, prattle of the Reverend Henry Green, a nineteenth-century minister of Brook Street Chapel and author of *Knutsford, its Traditions and History*. It is to be hoped that the Archaeological Society will spearhead a drive for a new appraisal and a re-writing.

Brook Street Unitarian Chapel is one of the few buildings now standing in Knutsford known to have been built prior to the eighteenth

century. Its founders were a Puritan community which had originated in
Civil War times and succeeded in holding together, like the similar
community at Ringway, during the persecution that followed the
Restoration. They wasted no time in taking advantage of the Toleration
Act of 1689; indeed, it seems possible that they anticipated it and had at
least begun the erection of their chapel before it was passed. They were, of
course, still Presbyterian in their beliefs and not Unitarians, for the
Unitarians were expressly excluded from the toleration permitted by the
new act. Their peaceful take-over of many of the chapels of the old
Nonconformity came in mid-eighteenth century, and was an illustration of
the extent to which the religious fanaticism of the preceding century had
withered away. Presbyterian or Unitarian, the Nonconformists had
neither the money nor the desire to be ostentatious and the charm of the
small brick-built chapel stems from its simplicity and modesty. Like the
parallel chapels at Dean Row, Wilmslow, and King Edward Street,
Macclesfield, it has small, square, two-light windows with latticed panes
and two external staircases leading to interior galleries. Mrs Gaskell,
whose husband was a Unitarian minister, although of Cross Street,
Manchester, and not of Brook Street, is buried in the graveyard.

Despite the lack of pre-eighteenth century buildings, the layout of the
centre of Knutsford is still that of an old town, the narrow winding King
Street having little alleyways leading away to the upper part of the town.
There are several gracious eighteenth-century houses within a stone's
throw of the dignified brick parish church of the 1740s. The most
remarkable building, however, the Gaskell Memorial Tower and King's
Coffee House, belongs to this century. It was built in 1907 by R. H.
Watt, a Manchester glove manufacturer, who employed his wealth and
leisure in getting a posse of architects to fulfil his notions of fine building.
He travelled much and his style – if it can be called a style – derived from
Spain, Southern Italy and Byzantium, and he even achieved, at the north
end of the town, a laundry which had eastern domes and a minaret. The
minaret survives. There is an incredible row of his villas in Legh Road.
His buildings exaggerate just those tendencies in Victorian architecture
against which Edgar Wood and the other professional architects of the
Arts and Crafts Movement were reacting. Yet the work of its freaks is as
much a memorial to a past age as anything else it leaves behind. It can
convey distinction upon a place and the shock of its first impact is

softened by the passage of time. Many Knutsfordians would regret the disappearance of the villas in Legh Road, now much threatened, and would furiously resist the removal of the Gaskell Tower. This commemorates Knutsford's most famous inhabitant in a way no passer-by can ignore and — although one imagines it would have been Watt's last consideration — fits in well with the rest of the street. The church stands back and is out of sight. All the other buildings are low. From either end the eye is drawn up to the white stone of the tower and if its outlines are irregular and asymmetrical, this suits well enough the windings and uneven levels of the street. Pride in his architectural achievements eventually caused Watt's death. He had a habit of standing up in his trap as he drove to the station, the better to view them. One day the horse shied; he was thrown out and fatally injured.

The plain west and north-west of Knutsford contained in former times many of the great country seats of notable Cheshire families. Almost all the families have now gone and many of the halls. Arley Hall, the second seat of the 'mighty Warburton', however, still has much of interest. A barn with seven cruck trusses survives that may well have been there in the days of the Warburtons who fought at Bosworth and Flodden. The Hall, a Jacobean-style brick mansion of the 1830s, and the model estate village with its timber-frame school at Arley Green, were put up by Rowland Egerton-Warburton who was lord of the manor for most of the nineteenth century. He was an improving landlord and a promoter of 'Merrie England', who revived the maypole and dancing on the village green at Arley. He was also the author of hunting songs and other occasional verse, some specimens of which can still be seen on signposts in the estate. The beautiful gardens of the Hall (open to the public at certain times) contain a herbaceous border that was one of the first to be established in the country. For herbaceous borders were one of the results of the spread of an interest in botany during the nineteenth century.

In Egerton-Warburton's time Great Budworth village was part of the Arley estate, and it was largely due to the squire of Arley that it has remained the charming village it is today. He saw to the preservation of many of the old cottages and the restoration or rebuilding of others in a style that preserved the former atmosphere. Much of the work was done by John Douglas, the Cheshire architect, who also designed many of the farms and hamlets on the Eaton estate of the Grosvenors.

Rising above the village on its hillock is the great church, once the centre of the largest parish in Cheshire, a county noted for large parishes. It contained 35 townships, reaching the Mersey near Warrington to the north and extending almost as far as Holmes Chapel to the south-east. The church looks its part. The stepped buttresses at the angles of its tall tower, the battlements that crown its nave, aisles, side chapels and south porch give it a suitable air of strength and dominance.

Across the north end of Knutsford's King Street stands the southern lodge of Tatton Park. Since the death of the last Lord Egerton in 1958 Park and Hall have been administered by Cheshire County Council for the National Trust, and in many years have been the most visited of all the Trust's properties. It is not difficult to see why, and it is not just because they are close to a conurbation. The Park and the gardens are both lovely and extensive. Terraces and sloping lawns fall away to Tatton Mere; the Pennines form a backcloth. Repton had a hand in the landscaping and, very probably, Paxton in the terracing. There is great. variety in the gardens: an. orangery, a New Zealand fernery, a rose garden, acres of rhodoendrons and azaleas, a beech avenue leading to a classical rotunda, a Japanese garden with a real Shinto temple. The Hall, built by Samuel Wyatt and his nephew, Lewis, between 1788 and 1820, is extensive but not overwhelming. One feels that it was designed, not so much to impress as to enable its owners to live a pleasant and cultured existence in it. The library, with its range of windows looking through the Corinthian pillars of the south front out over the terracing, lawns and shrubs to the Cheshire plain and the Pennines beyond, must be one of the loveliest settings for reading and meditation ever built. The house continued to be furnished and lived in up to the time of the last Lord Egerton's death. There is much of interest in it relating to Victorian times and after: the kitchens, a house list of the Golden Jubilee year when the Prince of Wales was a guest, a painting of the Manchester Ship Canal and the spade with which the Earl Egerton of the day cut the first sod of the canal (he was chairman of the Canal Board from 1887 to 1894), the last Lord Egerton's early motor cars, wireless sets and a huge collection of game trophies. The story comes right up to modern times and, as yet, there is little break with the past.

The. popularity of the eighteenth-century mansion has quite diverted attention from the Old Hall which lies almost a mile away. Now investigations have revealed that the timber building incorporated in it dates back to pre-Reformation days. So its great hall would have witnessed the feasts and public occasions of three of the great families who were at Tatton before the Egertons came, the Masseys, the Stanleys and the Breretons.

A mile or so to the north-west and the east of Tatton Park are two fine parish churches, Rostherne and Mobberley. Rostherne's position is striking, a little away from its village and high above Cheshire's largest and deepest mere. The mere, a formation of the immediate post-glacial age, is now a bird sanctuary. The surroundings are entirely rural and secluded, although they are almost within sight and sound of the M6 and only a few miles from the Manchester conurbation. The church is an odd combination. Neglect resulted in the west tower crashing down in 1740, and it and most of the nave had to be rebuilt. The result is curious but quite pleasing; dormer windows in the roof and a west door with pediment and pilasters at the foot of an otherwise medieval-looking tower. Some of the late medieval church remains in the south aisle but the chancel is Victorian.

It is recorded that in 1740 'the greatest school for teaching arithmetic and mathematics in the whole county' was held directly under the tower and escaped destruction by a couple of hours when the tower fell. The brief for the rebuilding said 'Tis happy for the town (i.e. township) that it fell in the evening . . . . the youths were gone home'. It might be thought that this was an understatement of their luck, for the wardens' accounts reveal that the condition of the tower was causing serious alarm nearly 40 years before. Why Rostherne should have had so distinguished a mathematics school is unknown, unless it harked back to Adam Martindale who was minister at Rostherne during the Commonwealth. His autobiography, published by the Chetham Society, is a fascinating account of the difficulties of a conscientious professional clergyman in times of religious near-anarchy. Having supported the Puritan cause against the 'tyranny' of the bishops and the Prayer Book, once these were abolished he was confronted by the zealots of his own side, some of whom regarded professional clergymen like himself and the whole organisation of a national church as just as great hindrances to true worship as bishop and Prayer Book had ever been. Martindale coped as best he could, but it was the Restoration and his subsequent ejection from

Rostherne that brought out his real intellectual capacity. Although he had not been brought up in an academic atmosphere (his father was a farmer-cum-builder from near Prescott), had had indifferent schooling, never gone to a university and was already middle-aged, he took up the study of mathematics. A revolution in method, even more profound than the one that has taken place recently, was in progress, but he took this in his stride, published papers which were approved by the new Royal Society and was employed by the High Master of Manchester Grammar School to coach his brightest pupils.

Although Mobberley is a long straggling village with a great deal of commuter housing, the church stands almost alone, only the rectory, an inn and a few cottages beside it. Chiefly late medieval, although with some fragments from earlier periods, its main glory is its woodwork. The rood screen, which has a date 1500 on it, is one of the finest in the county, covered with rich tracery in which geometric patterns, leaves and fruit, coats-of-arms and religious monograms are mixed. Above it is a 'cellure' roof (one especially constructed to go above the rood) and its more delicate transverse ribs and bosses contrast with the larger bosses and great camber beams of the main roof.

The area south of Knutsford was once dominated by the two branches of the Leicester family at Nether Tabley and at Toft, and, until very recently, both halls were still in the possession of members of the family. Neither is open to the public. The Leicesters of Tabley have a distinction unusual for members of the ancient Cheshire squirearchy: in the seventeenth, eighteenth and nineteenth centuries, the heads of the family were writers and patrons of the arts. Sir Peter Leicester, who built the little chapel now re-erected alongside the New Hall, was Cheshire's first historian, publishing in 1673 his *Historical Antiquities,* which contain a detailed study of the Hundred of Bucklow. His misfortunes were Cheshire's good fortune. His fervent royalism debarred him from all local office during the Commonwealth and gave him leisure for his researches. The first Lord de Tabley, who was born in 1762, the very year of the erection of the New Hall by the noted York architect, John Carr, became a great patron of the arts. In particular he encouraged Turner and, in the recent great Turner exhibition at Burlington House, there were several sketches and paintings of Tabley Hall. The third Lord de Tabley was a well-known Victorian man of letters. His fame now rests chiefly on his

Cheshire Flora. Here his scholarly nature and orderly mind led him to make a most comprehensive survey of the county's wild flowers at a time when urbanisation was only just beginning to be a threat. Today it is an invaluable, if rather melancholy, record of what we have lost. His verse, which had some reputation for a time after his death, is rather too steeped in aristocratic melancholy or too imitative of his greater contemporaries to be much read today, but it contains some fine lines, a few of which are on his tombstone in Lower Peover churchyard.

The church of Lower Peover first appeared as a chapel of ease in Great Budworth parish as far back as the thirteenth century. It is considered possible that some of the massive timber framing of the nave, the octagonal piers with great braces going across and along, could date back to this period. A stone west tower was added in Henry VII's day and, in mid-nineteenth century, Salvin replaced the original external timber frame of the church, which included nave and aisles under one roof, with another timber frame having three separate roofs. Fortunately he left most of the furnishings and there is a wealth of fine woodwork: a thirteenth-century dug-out chest, Jacobean screens, pulpit, lectern and pews.

The church stands at the end of a cobbled lane leading from a secondary road, is surrounded by woods and fields and has only a handful of buildings by it. One of these is the little brick two-storeyed parish school, founded by the vicar, Richard Comberbach, in 1710 and only very recently ceasing to function as a school. Another is the inn, the 'Bells of Peover', whose fame as a restaurant has made this secluded spot known to thousands. The name had nothing to do originally with the bells of the church, but derived from a licensee who was there so long that *Bell's* became common parlance among the locals. The official name during this period was the Warren de Tabley Arms.

If Lower Peover church is secluded, Over Peover church is almost out of the public eye altogether, approachable only by footpath and winding country lane. It is dominated by the nearby Hall which was once the chief seat of the ancient and important county family of the Mainwarings. Its insignificant eighteenth-century brick tower and early nineteenth-century brick nave are dwarfed by stone chapels erected by the Mainwarings in the fifteenth and seventeenth centuries. The Mainwaring effigies are the most interesting feature of the church, the plate armour of the fifteenth-century knights rivalling that of the Savages in their chapel in St Michael's, Macclesfield. Even more splendid is the armour of Philip Mainwaring of Civil War times, but it is likely that this would have been largely ornamental, even if Philip had not been the reluctant participant that he was. He was the only head of any of the great ancient families of Cheshire to take the parliamentary side; the probable cause of his action lies beside him with a plain kerchief about her head and her hands raised in prayer. His wife Ellen came from the strongly Puritan family of the Minshulls of Stoke near Nantwich. Philip led no troops into battle and became more and more disenchanted with the side he had chosen. The interesting reaction of their son, Thomas, to the whole situation is told in Chapter Ten, because he spent most of his time at the family's second country seat at Baddiley near Nantwich.

Nether Alderley church is almost as much of a family mausoleum as Over Peover, although it is twice the size, stands by a main road and was a parish church at least as far back as the fourteenth century. Monuments to the Alderley branch of the Stanleys are everywhere. In a sense this is fortunate as their old hall across the road was largely burnt down in 1779 and its successors have gone too, the modern buildings of an I.C.I. research division occupying their site. The Stanley pew in the church is elevated to first floor level in an arch of the nave arcade and provided with a private entrance from outside. This pew and the musicians' gallery at the west end of the church are covered with the shields of the Stanleys and related noble families. In the chancel, rebuilt by the Stanleys in Victorian times, are the effigies of the first and second Lord Stanleys of Alderley. The first was an author and member of the Royal Society who, in his youth, equipped and led what was probably the first scientific expedition from this country to Iceland. On his return he published an account of its hot springs. The second lord Stanley was a well-known politician in his day, serving in five mid-nineteenth century Liberal governments. There are memorials to other members of the family and, when these threatened to overflow the church, a mausoleum was erected in the churchyard. It stands just behind the little stone parish school, first put up by Hugh Shaw, curate of Alderley, in 1628 and enlarged by Edward Stanley, rector and brother of the first Lord Stanley, early in the nineteenth century.

Although, as mentioned earlier in this book, the Stanley ladies made a great fuss about preserving their seclusion against 'Cottentot' demands for special days to visit the Edge, it was one of them, an unmarried daughter of the first Lord Stanley, who stimulated public interest in the Edge by publishing a booklet about it which included the tale of the Wizard. This tells how a farmer was accosted on the Edge by an old man who offered him a price for his milk-white horse. The farmer refused, saying he could get a better price at Macclesfield fair. When he returned, having failed to do so, he was again met by the old man who, in the dusk of evening, seemed of more than mortal stature. Leading the now terrified farmer to a wall of rock, he struck it with his wand; iron gates appeared and flew open to reveal a great cavern, lined with armoured warriors and their milk-white steeds, all sleeping. One warrior had no horse and it was for him that the farmer's horse was required. The sleeping warriors would, so the wizard said, emerge in time of need, fight a great battle and save the country. The links with Merlin, Arthur and legends of sleeping warriors the world over are obvious.

Nor did the Stanleys prevent another action which helped to spread publicity. The local inn had a new sign painted representing 'The Wizard of the Edge'. The Stanley ladies were chiefly alarmed (or so they said) that, as the sign had no lettering, people might mistake it for the figure of Lord Stanley, grown something of a recluse and an eccentric in his old age. As the Edge, once a hunting ground for Mesolithic man and a source of minerals — copper, lead, cobalt — from Roman times until the nineteenth century, has become one of the most visited spots in Cheshire and is now National Trust property, the fame of the Wizard Inn has grown along with it. Today, however, it is a fashionable restaurant and no longer an inn.

South of Nether Alderley, close to the A34, is Capesthorne Hall, home of the Bromley-Davenports. A younger branch of the great Davenport family, they were established nearby at Marton and Woodford in the Middle Ages, but only came to Capesthorne after marriage with the previous owners, the Wards, early in the eighteenth century. Of the early Georgian house, which the last of the Wards built, only some walling at the back of the present house and the chapel survives. The present Hall, also in brick, is the work of two famous Victorian architects, Blore and Salvin, Salvin rebuilding that part of the Blore mansion which was destroyed by fire in 1861. Outside, Capesthorne presents an irregular

outline of Elizabethan-style turrets and gables. The interior is more
restrained and neo-classical, although some of the rooms have ornate
plaster ceilings and fireplaces. There is a wealth of portraits and *objets
d'art* brought back by members of the family from the Grand Tour. There
has been a great tradition of 'back-benching' in Capesthorne. The present
owner and his two predecessors sat in the House of Commons for a
combined total of 58 years but never held ministerial office. All have been
strong Conservatives. One of the crests worked into the roundels of the
balustrade on the main staircase, which was built in the 1860s, reveals
their political allegiance. The crest is the felon's head, assumed by the
Davenports because the head of their house was the chief forester of
Macclesfield Forest and had rights of summary justice over all
wrongdoers caught in the Forest. This particular felon, however, bears the
face of Mr Gladstone.

South of Capesthorne the little churches of Siddington and Marton
stand almost alone on hillocks alongside the A34. Founded in the late
Middle Ages by the lords of nearby halls which no longer exist, both
were in origin timber-and-wattle. Early in the nineteenth century those
who replaced Siddington's decaying nave with brick painted this black
and white to match the rest, and produced a zebra effect which at close
quarters is rather overpowering. Marton, however, kept not only her
timber frame but, much more unusually, her three-storeyed wooden belfry.
As recently as the 1950s there was discovered under layers of whitewash
on the western interior wall of the church a medieval Doom or
representation of the Last Judgement.

The outstanding building of this part of Cheshire, however, is neither
church, hall nor civic building. It is Manchester University's Radio
Telescope at Jodrell Bank. The five bowls which receive the radio waves
from outer space were built between 1952 and 1966. The first and
biggest is 250 feet in diameter and still the largest steerable radio
telescope in the world. It is this rather than its smaller and later
companions which delights the eye by bursting into sight at odd moments
and in unexpected places: alongside the railway track between Chelford
and Holmes Chapel, framed in a cleft near the village of Goostrey, rising
up from the flat land east of the A50 with the Pennines as a background.
In the strict sense it is not architecture, in that no architect designed it, but
it is a powerful reinforcement of the fifty-year-old argument of the

Functionalists that that which is constructed simply to work may be more beautiful than that which is deliberately designed to please the eye. Had it been there in their day they would surely have added it to the liners, airships and aeroplanes which they instanced to support their theory.

In less than half an hour one can pass from the Space Age to the beginnings of Christianity in the north-west. The late 8th-century crosses in her market place are not Sandbach's only claim to fame, though. In the seventeenth century, when it was not wise to show too much interest in the fate of the crosses which had been knocked down with the approval of many of the local squires, Sandbach was more noted for its strong ale. 'True dagger stuff', Webb called it (and one can guess what that meant). During the Civil War a royalist officer from Ireland wrote that his regiment had driven the enemy from *Sanbage,* 'a place famous for strong ale', but they had left not a drop behind in their quarters. The fame of it, though not the reality, was still there in Aikin's day, but neither he nor previous writers give us any inkling how or where it was made, whether in a brewery, the local inns or the surrounding farmhouses.

The salt fields, developed in the nineteenth century, really stop at Elworth, a mile to the west. But industrial fame has come to Sandbach through Fodens. The firm began in mid-nineteenth century as a foundry specialising in making stationary steam engines. From this it developed into providing steam thrashing machines and traction engines for the prosperous farming community at its doors. In the 1930s the firm went over to diesel engines and a second company named ERF (from the initials E. R. Foden) was founded which specialised in making commercial trucks and tractors. Both companies have gained international markets, but to the British public at large Fodens is best known from the fame of its brass band. This is but one result of the concern which the family (still very much involved in both businesses) has shown for the welfare of its employees.

To return to the crosses, two of them are mentioned in Elizabethan times as still standing in the market place. We presume they had been broken down by 1623 when Webb wrote, because he does not mention them and we know there had been much destruction of such 'idolatrous' symbols in the county in the intervening period. Probably their fragments lay about the market place for some time, smaller pieces being removed for building purposes. Parts of the main shafts were eventually carried off to serve as ornaments on various estates, until they came to rest in Oulton Park towards the end of the eighteenth century, when interest in such 'antiquities' was growing. An effort was made to bring together and re-erect the crosses, and interest in it was not confined to the squirearchy. Sir John de Grey Egerton of Oulton handed over the biggest fragments and gave the biggest subscription to the fund that was raised, but many others in the village and the surrounding countryside also subscribed and joined in the hunt for the remaining pieces. The search was supervised by no less a person than George Ormerod, author of the greatest history of the county, while John Palmer, a Manchester architect with antiquarian leanings, provided the expertise for the re-erection. The interest aroused was so great that this was sometimes hampered by the large crowds that gathered. So the problem, which confronts present-day *Rescue* archaeologists, of having to arouse public support yet restrain some of its manifestations, was not unknown in former times.

Although referred to as the Sandbach *crosses*, actually only the shafts have survived. It is likely that the crosses themselves were free-armed and curved like the one surviving at Ruthwell near Dumfries. The carvings which cover both shafts provide the main interest. Down one side of the larger shaft is a vine scroll with beasts in its branches, a symbol that is invariably on the great Northumbrian crosses further north. Of the many groups of figures only a few can be interpreted with any certainty. On the eastern side of the larger shaft is Christ on the cross with the sun and moon above him and the symbols of the four Evangelists, an angel, a lion, a calf and an eagle in between the arms of the cross. Below is the Nativity. There are possible explanations of other groups. The great figures standing on a kind of ladder on the north side of the same shaft, figures standing on a kind of ladder on the south side of the same shaft, may represent the descent of the Holy Spirit. John Palmer had an ingenious explanation that the busy little figures in compartments on the north and south side of the smaller cross were Mercian warriors accompanying their pagan leader, the Mercian prince Peada, on journeys to and from Northumbria, where he married the Christian princess, Alcheda. The objects they carried up were warlike swords and daggers; those they returned to Mercia with were peaceful staves. Unfortunately the experts say that there is no parallel for representation of this kind of scene on other crosses of this type, and that the Sandbach crosses are at least 100 years later than Peada's conversion. Yet the little figures cry out for explanation.

The stones now used in the base for the two upright shafts show that there was a third cross and other sculptured work besides. The style of the carving and the subjects employed link the Sandbach crosses to other work in the north Midlands done at the end of the 8th century. This was just after the close of the reign of Offa, Mercia's most powerful king. It looks very much as if Sandbach was an important religious centre on the north-western fringe of the Saxon kingdom of the Midlands in the days of its greatness and before the county of Cheshire existed.

EIGHT

Central Cheshire:
The Salt Towns

So far north and south do the Keuper Marls underlie the Cheshire plain that salt springs have broken out within a mile or so of the Lancashire and Shropshire borders. In the seventeenth century the Booths had salt works on their Dunham Massey estates. A hundred years earlier John Leland recorded how a part of a wooded hill near Combermere Abbey suddenly sank and a pit of salt water formed. But what followed revealed where the real centre of the salt interests lay. 'The abbat ther began to make salt, but the men of the wichis componid with the abbay that ther should be no salt made.'

Nantwich, Northwich and Middlewich were the principal *wiches* or salt towns at least as far back as the Domesday Survey. At the end of the seventeenth century Nantwich began to fade as a salt town and Winsford to develop. In the nineteenth century the field swung eastwards almost to Sandbach. But even with this eastwards swing the main area covered has never been more than 15 miles long and six or seven broad, spread across the valleys of the Weaver, the Dane and the Wheelock.

Recent excavations have revealed that there was vigorous production of salt at Middlewich in Roman times. North of the town at the beginning of King Street, undoubtedly an old Roman road, nineteenth-century antiquaries saw what they thought were the earthworks of a Roman fort. Later the site, which lay between the Trent and Mersey Canal and the railway, was largely covered by houses, but the recent demolition of many of these houses has made extensive excavation possible. No fort has been found, but instead the outlines of long, narrow, timber workshops and the remains of brine pits, of the

20 *The view from the hill fort at Helsby, showing the Mersey estuary and Weston Point in the distance.*

briquetage (framework) of fired clay for the heating of salt pans and of jars for the holding of brine. One jar had AMYRCA scratched on it, known to be the name for a solution of brine waste used throughout the Empire for cleansing purposes. Coins and fragments of pottery found reveal occupation to have lasted for almost the whole period of Roman rule in the north-west. Parallel excavations, which have taken place in Northwich on a site alongside the main road to Chester just after it has crossed the Weaver, have shown that here occupation was brief – from about A.D. 70-140 – and, as the nineteenth-century antiquaries thought, primarily military. A helmet was found and the outlines of the northern and western defences traced. The pattern would seem to be that the fort at Northwich was built during the sweeping Roman advance northwards in the reign of the Emperor Vespasian. The first of the forts at Chester was built about the same date. Simultaneously a mushroom industrial town sprang up at Middlewich, on the site of a Celtic brine spring, to supply the Roman armies with salt. With the stabilisation of the Roman occupation behind the lines of the Hadrianic and Antonine Walls the fort became unnecessary and was abandoned, but the salt town continued in order to supply the needs of the new military and civilian communities in the area. One further result of these excavations has been to reverse the old nineteenth-century naming of the sites. *Condate (at the confluence –* presumably of the Weaver and the Dane) is now favoured for Northwich and *Salinae (the saltworks)* for Middlewich.

Whether or not the Romans produced salt at Northwich and Nantwich (where Roman settlement is unproven), all three Cheshire *wiches* were well established by the time of the Domesday Survey. The Tudor travellers and topographers made them known nationally. Leland, Camden and others described the process of salt making: the drawers bringing the brine in buckets from the pits and pouring it into wooden troughs, the troughs conveying it to the 'leads' or pans in the salt houses, fires being lit under the leads and women called 'wallers' raking the salt from the boiling water into wicker baskets from which the surplus liquid drained off. Vast quantities of wood were required and much smoke and dirt resulted. 'A prati [pretty] market toune but fowle' ('pretty' then meaning thriving), was Leland's description of Northwich, and this remained a fair enough assessment of the salt towns for many centuries afterwards.

21, 22 and 23 Three misericords from Nantwich church: wrestlers, the Devil pulling a woman's mouth open, and three portraits, perhaps Richard II and two of his master craftsmen.

Despite their growth, the salt *wiches* remained tiny industrial enclaves in purely rural surroundings. As late as the early seventeenth century Middlewich was simply a triangle of houses round its great church with one street running southwards, Northwich half a dozen short streets in an angle made by the confluence of the Dane with the Weaver. Nantwich, for reasons unconnected with salt, was rather larger. The complex set-up which controlled these towns, including the Crown (which drew profits from taxing salt), noble landowners, monastic houses and comparatively humble resident townsmen, restricted growth. There were involved rules limiting the times when boiling of salt was permissible. The salt owners not only wished to restrict profits to themselves, they feared that supplies of timber and of the brine itself might run out. They had no idea of the nature and extent of the salt field which underlay Cheshire. Furthermore once local needs had been supplied, wider markets were restricted by inadequate means of communication. As we have seen, Cheshire had virtually no waterways. Salt was conveyed locally by farmers, glad to use their draught animals and waggons for additional profit in seasons when they were not fully employed on their farms. For wider distribution there were salt merchants with their trains of pack-horses whose arduous routes, frequently not coinciding with the normal roads, can now only be guessed at by scattered names. There are Salterswall west of Winsford, Saltersford east of Holmes Chapel, Saltersbrook and Saltersbridge near Tarvin and, high up in the Pennines, another Saltersford at the Jenkin Chapel behind Macclesfield and another Saltersbrook on the Woodhead Pass over into Yorkshire.

Nothing remains above ground of the medieval salt *wiches* but their fine churches. Change and growth began towards the end of the seventeenth century. Shortage of timber began a hunt for coal near to the salt towns themselves. The result was the discovery in 1670, on the Marbury estate close to Northwich, not of coal but of rock salt. Despite an initial outcry against the quality of this new form of salt, it quickly established itself. It was bulky, however, and required much fuel to refine it. So the provision of transport to bring coal to the salt mines or the rock salt to the coal mines became crucial. At this time, also, the merchants of Liverpool were searching their hinterland for exports to balance the imports flooding in from across the Atlantic. Backed by the rock salt men, but opposed by the brine salt men, the landlords and the tenants who had provided the old waggon transport, it took the Liverpool men 20 years to get an act through Parliament to make the Weaver navigable. After this had been done in 1721, it took them a further ten years to jog the Cheshire landowners, to whom Parliament had given control of the new venture, into building it, and a further 20 to get the management reorganised so that proper repairs and improvements were ensured. But by 1763 the annual tonnage of goods carried on the Navigation, which had been 19,000 tons in 1733, the first full year of its operation, had jumped to 76,000 tons, and what had been thought of by many as a nuisance had become a valuable asset. A very wide range of goods came upstream to balance all the salt that went down.

There was great panic in the 1760s that the two new canals, the Bridgewater and the Grand Trunk, would by their junction destroy the trade of the Navigation and desperate, but unavailing, attempts were made to prevent this. The great growth of trade and industry, however, provided enough work to keep all the new waterways busy. Steam power brought yet further growth to the salt industry. Pumping kept the brine salt method going and boring instruments penetrated to deeper beds of rock salt.

Before 1700 there is no record of anyone, whether he was the Earl of Derby or 'Mr Horton of Cow Lane, Northwich', making a fortune through salt. Possession of a salt house was simply a useful addition to one's income. The history of the Marshall family in the eighteenth and early nineteenth century reveals the change that had come about. Thomas Marshall, the younger son of a textile worker, moved from the stagnating atmosphere of Nantwich early in the eighteenth century to seek opportunity in the expansion of Northwich. When he died in 1772 he owned brine and rock salt works and was shipping more salt down the Navigation than any other Northwich salt producer. When his son, also Thomas, died in 1797, *he* owned the vast Dunkirk mine where borings went down 300 feet to the lower salt level, a St Helens' coal mine, a fleet of 'flats' on the Navigation, a counting house in Liverpool and houses and shops in Northwich. His sons, John (died 1833) and Thomas (died 1831), attended assiduously to the business, organising a Salt Traders' Association to try and combat the growing problem of over-production. But their interests had widened; they served in the militia and on turnpike trusts, and donated large sums for the building of a church in Hartford, a pleasant village outside Northwich where they both now lived. John made additions and alterations to the eighteenth-century house which his father had bought and called Hartford Manor. Thomas built a charming new house at Hartford Beech with 'Gothick' porch, iron balcony and bay windows. They filled their homes with beautiful furniture, silver, china and paintings. Both their houses still stand; John's is now the offices of the local Gas Board. Following generations, the descendants of Thomas the younger brother, lost interest in the business and finally broke with it. They were educated at the major public schools, had military careers, fished, hunted and shot with the aristocracy and even with royalty. They acquired property and built residences in North Wales. Although they continued to own large estates in Cheshire until the twentieth century, they had moved right out of both its industrial and its social life.

The development of the salt trade had other results besides the production of family fortunes. As Leland's account of the sudden disappearance of a hill at Combermere makes plain, there had always been subsidence. But the new minings and pumpings and the discovery that brine salt could be pumped out of abandoned mine workings that had been naturally or artificially flooded produced its occurrence on an undreamt-of scale. On the night of 16 October 1838 the top level of the Ashton Mine, whose bottom level was still being worked, caved in, engulfing the engine house and 12 workmen. Not long afterwards a gentleman awoke to find that his fruit garden had dropped 100 feet during the night. Investigations revealed that the mine whose collapse had caused the drop was the original Marbury mine of 1670, which had been closed and its whereabouts forgotten somewhere about the middle of the eighteenth century. The photographs at the back of Calvert's monumental *History of Salt in Cheshire* are a vivid testimony of what followed. They show shops, offices and private residences, some tilted at crazy angles, some with their ground floor or even first floor windows below street level, some lifted on stilts, some nothing more than a pile of rubble. There are roads with huge cracks across their surfaces, craters full of water and even sizable 'flashes' where not a pond had stood before.

By 1870 the cries for compensation were attracting national attention. So unusual were the circumstances, however, so complicated the legal niceties and so powerful the opposition of the salt owners, that it was not for another 20 years that an act was passed setting up a compensation fund to be raised from a rate on all brine pumping in the Northwich area.

In 1874 when John Horatio Marshall, Eton and Sandhurst, was objecting to being 'named as a salt manufacturer' and selling the family works to the Salt Union, a new era was beginning for the industry. The year before Ludwig Mond and John Brunner had opened their works at Winnington Hall for the making of soda by a new process. The old sulphur process had been established at Runcorn and Widnes for some time and both partners had had experience of it. It was noted for the devastation it caused to the vegetation for miles around and its appalling smell. The new Winnington works did not entirely get rid of the smell and Mrs Mond had to keep the windows of the old Tudor-cum-Georgian Hall shut. For the fantastic-looking works that were now arising virtually sprouted out of the Hall, as her husband wanted to be able to dash from one to the other at any hour of the day or night. It was, as his partner said later, a period when 'Everything that could break down did break down and everything that could burst did burst.' Mechanical failures were not their only trouble, for it was a time of trade depression and they had begun on a capital of no more than £20,000, most of it borrowed. However, once trade picked up and the new ammonia process proved to be cheaper and more efficient, as well as cleaner, than the old sulphur process, the shares of Brunner Mond quintupled. Mond, whose passion was for scientific research while his partner provided the business acumen, commented, almost with a note of disgust, 'We are no longer making chemicals, we are making money.'

If the Winnington works and a second which appeared at Lostock Gralam did not re-beautify the already somewhat devastated Northwich landscape, at any rate Brunner's boast, 'I have done more for Cheshire than all the Brookes and all the Mainwarings ... My friend Dr Mond and I have filled more hungry stomachs and founded more happy homes', was not without foundation. Brunner Mond's record as benevolent employers was impressive. They were one of the first firms to give their employees annual holidays with pay, they positively encouraged them to join a union, they required their apprentices to attend evening classes until they were 19 and paid their fees for them, they built model homes in the (then) countrified surroundings of Weaverham village. In addition, Brunner was an enthusiast for the extension of education. He had new schools built at Winnington and Barnton and added to the endowments of Sir John Deane's, Northwich's old grammar school, on the condition that a new wing for the teaching of girls should be added to it.

Now chemical works, those of I.C.I. (the giant successor to Brunner Mond) and others, greatly outnumber salt works in mid-Cheshire and the only salt mine continuing to operate is that at Meadow Bank, Winsford. Producing mainly for road-gritting, it has underground roads big enough for full-sized lorries to use and equipped with road signs, roundabouts and traffic lights. Modern methods of pumping and laying long pipe lines mean that refining works need no longer be on top of the salt fields. I.C.I.s great pumping station at Holford, south of Knutsford, supplies brine to works as far away as Weston Point, Runcorn and Widnes. The chemical industries of Cheshire think that they have now found a method to end the danger of subsidence, already grown much rarer since the 1920s. This is called *controlled* pumping. Cavities are made deep in the salt beds, water is injected and the salt removed by solution. The extent of these cavities is pre-determined and, as they are made below the level at which natural brine forms, it is said that there is no danger of them spreading and linking up with each other.

There are still plenty of relics of the unrestrained days of Cheshire's most distinctive industry. What were once the sites of the great salt mines – Dunkirk, Ashton's, Neumann's – reveal themselves in hummocks to the north of the Witton-Northwich road and the stretches of water used for many years for dumping the waste products of the chemical industry. Nevertheless a great effort is being made to tidy up. This has gone farthest in Winsford, a creation of eighteenth-century growth, whose salt production reached its height in the middle of the nineteenth century. With an additional 'overflow' from Liverpool and no longer dependent on salt alone, it has placed a number of new industries on a neat trading estate and built itself a new shopping centre and a civic hall. One of its most interesting, if slightly ironic, developments is the attempt to turn to good advantage the legacy of subsidence by converting its once dreary Top and Bottom Flashes into recreation centres. Flashes near Sandbach have produced another type of compensation already. The soil and water unwittingly created by man's industrial activities have attracted new species of flora and rare wading birds. Planners have now taken up what was originally quite unplanned and the flashes are scheduled as nature reserves.

Nature, in fact, has never been, and still is not, far from the industrial enclaves of mid-Cheshire. Edward I picked Vale Royal as a quiet and remote spot for the devotions and meditations of his new monastic foundation. There are not even any ruins left of his great Cistercian abbey, although excavations — now covered over — revealed its church to have been the longest and most elaborate of all the Cistercian abbey churches in England. But the vast house of the Cholmondeleys, built on its ruins and recently occupied by a succession of business enterprises and local authorities, stands in a still secluded spot alongside a little used stretch of the Weaver Navigation. It is difficult to grasp that this quiet spot lies between Northwich and Winsford and less than three miles from the centre of each.

NINE

Central Cheshire: Highland and Forest

If the traveller crosses the Weaver at or near Northwich and carries on westwards, he soon becomes aware that he is entering a different countryside. The roads dip and rise more often and more steeply, and rounded hills appear to left and right. If he is on the train, it will plunge into defiles lined by coniferous trees. He is, at one and the same time, in the central highlands of Cheshire and the area that once was Delamere Forest. In prehistoric times it was the most thickly inhabited part of a very thinly inhabited region; in the Middle Ages the progress of agriculture and, with this the growth of population, was arrested by the imposition of forest laws. To this day it has no towns and only a few large villages.

The remains of six of Cheshire's seven known hill forts lie within it; a northern group of Helsby, Woodhouses and Bradley and a southern group of Eddisbury, Kelsborrow and Oakmere. They are the work of Iron Age men, although the origins of some may well go back into the Bronze Age. Not all the forts are actually on hills. Bradley and Oakmere utilise water defences, the first a stream, the second a mere. But all have a similar pattern of using natural obstacles as a basis on which to build ramparts and ditches. An angle or promontory of land with steep slopes or even precipices is cut off by a rampart and ditch on the third side. The flattened top of a hill is completely enclosed by ramparts and ditches. The amount of ground enclosed varies from a few acres to fifteen, and the defences themselves from the sketchy to the elaborate. A full-scale excavation of Eddisbury, the largest of the forts, from 1935-8 revealed that those who built it had some knowledge of engineering and must have controlled a well-organised labour force. Their ramparts had stone revetments and in some places timber interlaced with the clay in the cores. The two entrances had cobbled roadways, the western one with the easier gradient bearing the marks of wheels, the eastern one showing remains of two gateways and stone-built guardrooms.

The Cheshire forts are a mere handful compared with the number contained in some counties on the Welsh border and in the south-west. Whom they belonged to at the time of the Roman invasion is not known with any certainty and only Eddisbury has yielded any evidence as to its fate. There are quarry-dressed stones packed neatly into its ditches with a Roman-type tile among them. As there are no traces of conflict, it looks as if the surrender must have been peaceful. Little has been found in any of the Cheshire forts revealing the way of life of the inhabitants or even how they made use of the forts, whether as permanent habitations or purely as refuges in time of danger.

Hill fort sites are pleasant places to visit on a fine day, the air bracing, the views often extensive. Two warnings may be given about them, however. All the Cheshire ones except Helsby, which is National Trust property, are on private lands and the owner's or tenant's permission should be sought before visiting them. He is under no obligation whatsoever to give it, particularly to the casual viewer. Nor do hill forts render up their secrets on sight to the uninitiate. It is true that the long flat top of Eddisbury Hill as seen from Delamere Station or on the right hand of the A556 looks artificial, and is. In fact the viewer may be seeing, not only the work of the Iron Age men, but the 914 rebuilding by Ethelfelda's *burh-men*, for according to the *Anglo-Saxon Chronicle* she established a fort at Eddisbury in this year. It is not possible, however, for the uninformed layman to go much further than this on his own. All the excavations have, of course, been filled in. What look like ramparts may be natural banks, and smooth slopes may conceal complex entrances. The prospective viewer would be well advised, therefore, to look first at J. Forde-Johnston's survey of all the Cheshire and Lancashire hill forts in the *Transactions of the Lancashire and Cheshire Antiquarian Society* and W. J. Varley's detailed account of the 1935-8 excavations at Eddisbury in the *Transactions of the Historic Society of Lancashire and Cheshire.*

The plateau of Eddisbury terminates in a little spur known as Merrick's Hill. Its tangled vegetation caused great trouble to the archaeologists, but they succeeded in establishing that it was within the original hill fort and contained the remains of medieval drainage and four buildings dating from the late Middle Ages to the eighteenth century. These discoveries confirm it as the site of the *Chamber in the Forest*, referred to in medieval documents and shown on early maps of the county. This was really a kind of operational headquarters for the chief-forester, deputy for the earl in the administration of Delamere Forest. Although Saxon kings and earls had their hunting grounds, the reservation of great areas of the country for their sport was a policy devised by the Norman monarchs. In Cheshire the forests were originally the earl's and not the king's, another instance that Cheshire was 'different'. Delamere, the largest of the three Cheshire forests, was in the first instance the twin forests of Mara and Mondrem. Mara lay north-west and Mondrem south-east of *Peytefinsty*, a medieval road running along the line of the A49. The origin and meaning of *Peytefin* has so far defied the place-name experts, but *sty* was the word the Saxons employed for a way which was not a *straet*, a term they reserved for old Roman roads.

We have more information about Delamere Forest than we have about the forests of Macclesfield and the Wirral. At its greatest extent it stretched from the southern end of Frodsham marsh almost to Nantwich and from the Weaver to the Gowy. It was not, of course, all wooded. In the 1530s Leland noted, besides 'sumwhat hilly and wooddy grounde', 'plaine blake hethi grounde'. Manors with sizable villages, even towns, could be included in it. At one time and another Frodsham, Tarvin, Tarporley and Weaverham were all in Delamere Forest. There were areas for pasturage and even for arable. But once an area was declared to be forest, the primary concern of those in charge of it became the preservation of 'the beasts of the chase', that is the three varieties of deer and the fast disappearing boar. Therefore regulations were imposed forbidding the harming of the beasts even if they were destroying crops, or the injuring of vegetation (which gave them cover) by the pasturing of domestic animals. Household dogs had to be *lawed* (i.e. lamed) so that they might not jump at the deer; the carrying of bows and arrows was always restricted, sometimes forbidden. Killing or injuring the beasts could be punished by death or mutilation. These regulations and such ordinary laws as remained were enforced by special courts, the most dreaded of which was the 'Forest Eyre', where travelling justices of king or earl judged major offences.

Increasing afforestation met growing protests in England and in Cheshire. The barons of Magna Carta forced King John to issue a Charter of the Forests. At about the same time Ranulf III, Earl of Chester, inserted clauses concerning the forests in his separate charter to his Cheshire barons. Very reluctantly king and earl were forced to halt the growth of afforestation and limit punishments to fines and imprisonment.

In the long run it is probable that the growing demand for land for agricultural use had even more effect than the protests of the barons. In Cheshire this was assisted by the almost perpetual absence of the earls once the Crown had taken over. After Edward I, James I is the only royal earl who is known to have hunted in Delamere Forest, and that for one day only. *Assarting,* the ploughing up of forest land for agricultural purposes, had become so common in Delamere Forest by the time of the Black Prince that his officials merely concerned themselves with imposing enormous fines for it. The inhabitants replied by resisting payment by all the means at their disposal. This apparently included the threat of rebellion, for in 1353 the Prince and other great nobles brought an army to overawe the county. Yet, throughout the dispute, the Prince and his officials never suggested that the illegally assarted land must be restored to the beasts of the chase. By the time of Charles I even the chief forester himself, Sir John Done of Utkinton, was petitioning that he would willingly surrender the perquisites of his office (he got no salary for it) in return for a grant of land at 'a place called the old Pale where I was born'. It is obvious from this that by this time the Dones regarded the Chamber of the Forest, which was the centre of the Old Pale, as much as a family residence as Utkinton Hall itself.

The end came in 1812, when what was left of the medieval forest was officially disafforested. The Crown retained some land and much of this is still farmed as crown property. The rest was allotted to private owners. Some of the crown lands were reserved under the Surveyor of Woods and Forests (now the Forestry Commission) and planted with conifers. This was the foundation of the small modern Forest of Delamere which lies north-west and north-east of Delamere station. Serving a quite different purpose from its predecessor, it has of recent years welcomed visitors to its precincts, instead of debarring them. A very pleasant time can be spent walking and picnicking in it, yet its orderly and predominantly coniferous growth gives little idea of what a medieval hunting preserve would have looked like. Nevertheless those times have left their imprint. In the heart of the old forest land there are not only no towns, but no villages of any size, no old halls and no old churches. There are not even the sites or the memory of old churches. Delamere parish church was built in 1816 on land set aside in the disafforestation of 1812. The churches at Kingsley, Norley, Crowton and Alvanley did not appear until after 1850.

On the fringes of Delamere Forest, where it was easier to gain exemption from its restrictions, towns and large villages, churches and manor houses did grow up. There was a church at Weaverham at the time of Domesday; the present structure dates mostly from the late Middle Ages and has a fine west tower and a broad nave and aisles. By the time it was built its patronage and tithes had been granted to the abbot of nearby Vale Royal, who had his court house in the village. Weaverham, therefore, must have been the centre point of the amazing struggle that took place between the abbot and the villeins of the abbey's manor of Darnhall in the fourteenth century, not many years before the Peasants' Revolt. The villeins contended that they were free men and not the abbot's bondsmen. As might be expected they lost their case, but what is astonishing is that they maintained it for so long, forced the justiciar in Chester to try it, travelled all over the country and had audiences of the king and the queen in pursuance of it. We get just a hint of the kind of backing that they must have had to accomplish all this, lay landholders who had quarrelled with the abbey over other matters. Ormerod gives us a glimpse of the village in the early nineteenth century, with its narrow streets and timber buildings separated from each other by little courts and gardens. A few of these buildings and a little of the atmosphere remain near the church to this day, but since Brunner Mond began building their model cottages there Weaverham has increasingly become a suburb of Northwich.

At the other end of the old Forest area is Tarvin, a sleepy little village as late as the 1950s, now fast becoming, if not a suburb of Chester, at least a desirable haven for some of its commuters. Tarvin was one of the larger Cheshire manors at the time of Domesday and the centre of a big parish by the fourteenth century. The present church was begun at this time and contains much fourteenth-century work, including the single-framed, arch-braced roof of the south aisle, the oldest surviving timber roof in Cheshire. A great rebuilding of the church was begun in the late fifteenth century but never completed, possibly because of shortage of funds. The result is odd. From the road the church presents a most imposing front, a massive west tower with a fine ogee-arched doorway. From the rear, however, the wide east end of the north aisle with its heavily battlemented parapet completely dwarfs and outfaces the little gable ends of the nave and south aisle.

Inside and outside the church there is evidence of Tarvin's unsought hour of eminence. Bullet marks spatter the walls around the west door. A brass by the chancel in memory of a former mayor of Chester actually had a bullet in it until an acquisitive visitor prized it out. The elaborate but rather clumsy nave roof, with its hammer beams and carved brackets, was put up in 1650 to replace one damaged in the Civil War. We know there was a brisk cavalry engagement around the church in August 1644 and a few weeks later Sir William Brereton arrived, surrounded the village with earth ramparts and put a garrison into it. He was about to undertake the siege of Chester and needed an operational headquarters nearer to it than his previous one at Nantwich. For several months most of Brereton's correspondence to Parliament itself, to military headquarters in London and to the other Roundhead generals in the field was dated from Tarvin, and it was to Tarvin that their replies came. About a year later their capture of the eastern suburbs of Chester gave Brereton's army a forward H.Q. even nearer to their objective, and Tarvin's national importance vanished.

Although once within the bounds of the Forest, Tarvin is well out of the central highlands, on the stretch of the Manchester-Chester road that leaves the highlands by the Kelsall Gap and runs down to Stamford Bridge over the Gowy, the *stane* or stony ford of Saxon times. The motor age has brought traffic swirling about Tarvin nowadays, and resulted in a notable bottleneck in the narrow defile, two miles in length and lined with houses, at Kelsall. A mile or so south-west of Tarvin, approachable only by very narrow country roads, are the three little bridges known as Hockenhull Platts, a reminder of a traffic problem of an earlier age. Of stone and brick with cobbled surfaces, the middle bridge spans the Gowy itself, the side ones are for flood waters. They are sometimes referred to as 'pack-horse bridges', but to call them this is to miss their significance.

Webb's statement shows clearly that in 1623 they were 'the passage over our said Water *in our great London roadway*'. He thought that it would have been 'a great and charitable work' to have made a 'bridge for carts ... when the river riseth', but we know from later maps that this was never done. Wheeled traffic continued to make a long detour and cross the Gowy by a ford, even after the road had been turnpiked in 1743 and the coaching age had begun in earnest. Not until the 1770s was the official Chester-London road re-routed through Tarvin and the Hockenhull Platts allowed to relapse into obscurity.

Five miles south of Tarvin the Chester-London road is joined by the A49, the old *Peytefinsty,* just as it enters the Tarporley Gap between the central highlands and their southern extension, the Peckforton Hills. Tarporley village is described by Leland as 'a long pavid village or *thoroug fare*' and, even today, there is little of it that is not alongside the main road. This being so, it is not surprising that its most famous building is an inn, the Swan. Just before this was rebuilt in 1769, it became the meeting place of the exclusive Tarporley Hunt Club whose handful of founder members included a Mainwaring, a Crewe, a Cotton, a Wilbraham and a Cholmondeley. This soon became and has remained a dining rather than a hunt club, although for hunting men. Shortly after the founding of the Hunt Club racing began at Tarporley and flourished on a variety of sites until the Second World War. Before it ended, polo was started. Thus in one form or another the riding of the horse for sport and pleasure has remained the passion of the farmers and the landowners of the Tarporley district, although almost all the old squires have been replaced by new men, their wealth built up from modern industry. The splendour of their twentieth-century houses and gardens equals that of the old halls.

The disappearance of the greatest old hall in the district has meant the appearance of an entirely modern form of racing in this part of Cheshire. The Egertons of Oulton rebuilt their ancient hall in the eighteenth century and surrounded it by a magnificent park. In the early nineteenth century Sir John de Grey Egerton and his nephew and heir, Sir Philip, were men of learning and culture. They made a great collection of pictures, books and manuscripts at Oulton Hall, and donated antiquities which they had acquired to the British Museum. (As already mentioned, Sir John played a major part in the re-erection of the ancient crosses at Sandbach.) Then in

February 1926 a fire, probably started by an electrical fault, destroyed the Hall. The collapse of a burning ceiling killed seven people, who were amongst those trying to save the pictures, and the library, as yet untouched, had to be left to the flames. The Hall was not rebuilt and during the Second World War the park became a military camp and was covered with huts. Then, in 1952, the family leased part of it to a firm which owned a number of racing circuits including Brand's Hatch. The Cheshire Car Circuit, Oulton Park, was established, and can attract as many as 60,000 spectators on a Bank Holiday afternoon to this hitherto quiet corner of Cheshire.

TEN

South-Eastern Gateway

Cheshire's central highlands left behind, the Tarporley Gap widens into the Midland Gap, the 20-mile stretch dividing the end of the Pennines from the hummocky moraine land of northern Shropshire. Even now, when the physical obstacles on either side of it are no longer formidable, it remains the main communications channel between the North-west and the Midlands and London. The M6 has been constructed along it, as was the Grand Junction Railway in the nineteenth century and the Grand Trunk Canal in the eighteenth. Before that there was Webb's, 'our great London roadway' from Chester and Drunken Barnaby's route from further north. This explains why the apparently dissimilar parts of the one urbanised district in the whole area have, in fact, the same basic reason for their existence. There is not a single building in Crewe that was put up before the 1840s. Nantwich, now joined to Crewe by housing development, has over a hundred buildings listed as worthy of preservation for historical or architectural reasons. Crewe owes its existence to a station planted in purely rural surroundings by the directors of the first long-distance railway in Britain. Nantwich is thought of as in origin a salt town. But Nantwich's superiority over Northwich and Middlewich prior to the eighteenth century was not so much due to better salt as to better communications.

Because it was such a excellent centre, the directors of the Grand Junction Railway thought of it first as the site for the watering place their thirsty little engines must have somewhere in the Midland Gap. Even at this early stage they were aware that if they chose the right spot it might well develop into a junction. Authority in Nantwich, however, was long

24 above *Lyme Hall: Leoni's south front.* 25 below *The south front of Tatton Hall: the terracing is probably by Paxton.*

established and very conservative. It listened readily to the propaganda of the Birmingham and Liverpool Canal Company, at that very moment pushing its earthworks forward to join the network of canals just north of the town. The breath of the locomotives, they said, was 'as poisonous as that of the fabled dragons of old . . . If a bird flew over the district where one of these engines passed, it would inevitably drop dead.' So the directors went to the rural townships east of Nantwich, where land was cheaper, a renegade farmer was already prepared to sell, and the local authorities too petty and divided to put up much opposition.

The image of Crewe in the public mind has not been kindly. As Webb said of Neston in the early seventeenth century, many people have been 'better acquainted with this place than they desire to be'. Waiting for a train replaced waiting for a wind and the process, if less lengthy, could be just as frustrating.

> *Oh! Mister Porter, what shall I do? –*
> *I want to go to Birmingham and they're taking me on to Crewe.*

Not many stranded passengers ever left the vast railway station to see the sights of the town, and those that did were not well rewarded. I myself remember an afternoon and evening spent in Crewe many years before I came to live in Cheshire. A walk from the station in one direction in search of the centre struck no more than a gaggle of buses surrounded by a few pubs and a cinema. A walk in the other direction – it was by this time dark – plunged me suddenly and totally into a thinly populated countryside.

Yet its inhabitants have always been rather proud of Crewe. After all it is the one and only railway town. Possible rivals turn out, like Darlington, to have been towns with a long history before locomotives were ever invented or, like Swindon, to have grown large and developed other interests. In the case of Crewe, however, not even a hamlet preceded the town established by the railway company and, although Rolls-Royce and other industries have come to it, the railway still dominates. The only outstanding modern building in the town is the 13-storey administrative block, the Rail House, and a recent broadcast revealed that in 1974 the last mayor of the old municipal borough and most of the council were railwaymen.

26 above *Some of the 2nd Earl of Warrington's great trees in Dunham Park.* 27 below
  The Grosvenor Bridge: St Mary's, Handbridge, seen through Thomas Harrison's great arch.

The directors of the Grand Junction had not intended to build a town themselves, and neither the stopping place which they set up on their original line in 1837, nor even the junction which their join-up with the Birmingham and Manchester and Chester and Crewe Railways had produced by 1842 necessitated this. It was the moving to Crewe in 1843 of their engine sheds and repair and construction workshops from Edgehill outside Liverpool which did. It increased the numbers of drivers and firemen who would have to live in Crewe and added to them engine and coach builders, all highly skilled workers whose labour the company could ill afford to lose and who were accustomed to living in an established urban community. The chairman of the directors said with perfect sincerity to the 900 workpeople at the ceremony held to mark the move that he and his brother directors were 'anxious to make them as comfortable as lay within their power'.

So they built neat cottages with four 'apartments' for the lowest paid and detached 'mansions', each housing four families, for the more highly skilled. When further amalgamations converted the Grand Junction into the L.N.W.R., this continued the role of benevolent employer and Crewe soon got gas, piped water, well-paved streets and, as the old parish church of Church Coppenhall was outside the town, the new parish church of Christ Church with school attached. The company also provided a doctor and a surgery and ran a health insurance scheme for its employees.

It may be asked why, if there was this enlightened paternalism, Crewe is not as impressive to look as are Port Sunlight and Bourneville. The answer is that the railway company, not having set out to plan a community, as had W. H. Lever and the Cadburys, but simply having made a virtue of necessity, grew alarmed when they saw that they were getting involved in running an entire town. From the 1860s on they transferred control of housing, public buildings and other amenities to the new local Board of Health. Yet, because they felt they must guard against any development that might threaten their own interests, they did not leave direction of the town's affairs entirely alone, and inevitably their employees tended to dominate its councils. In some instances, too, the company's past benevolence actually hindered progress. As the company had set up public baths in 1845, the local authority built no new ones until 1937. Because from the beginning the company had provided a doctor in a makeshift hospital, there were makeshift hospitals in houses and cottages until 1900. Crewe became a borough in 1877, but the municipality used all sorts of borrowed premises (most of them railway property) until 1902, and the then new Town Hall was so cramped by shops and small property that it was almost invisible. (In my odyssey of the 1930s, although I must have been within a stone's throw of it, I missed it entirely.) Now that the recent Civic Centre scheme has given it some space and other public buildings to set it off, it is shown to be pleasant and dignified.

Although only 130 years old, Crewe has little left of its beginnings. The old engine sheds have gone, the station has been rebuilt out of all recognition, only one of the four-family mansions remains in Prince Albert Street and a few of the cottages in and about Dorfold Street. Even the original Christ Church of 1843 has been largely obliterated by later additions and rebuildings. Too recently and too late has it been realised that the origins of so youthful a town could have their interest.

By contrast Nantwich is undoubtedly very old. Although no Roman site has ever been discovered there, frequent finds of coins, weapons and tools make Roman settlement probable, and the long entry in Domesday Book reveals that its importance as a salt town was established well back in Saxon times. By the end of the Middle Ages it was clear that, although without walls, royal charter or corporation, Nantwich was becoming Cheshire's second town. That it occupied this position in the early seventeenth century is obvious from Webb's comments on it and the attitude of both sides towards it during the Civil War. Both regarded it as the only possible alternative headquarters to Chester in the county, and Brereton's capture of it on the day after he returned from Westminster in January 1643 was the foundation of his later success.

The parish church of St Mary's is the only building surviving from medieval Nantwich. Although at the time only a chapel of the church of Acton, a mile to the west of the town, it is a sufficient witness to the importance and prosperity of the town and has been called the 'Cathedral of South Cheshire'. Built mostly in the fourteenth and fifteenth centuries, it has transepts and a splendid octagonal tower over the crossing. It is rich in relics of medieval practices of worship: in the chancel a piscina, an aumbry and a sedilia, all well preserved and the last two having richly carved canopies. No other church in Cheshire, not even the cathedral, shows so strongly the splendour of medieval carving in stone and wood.

Outside there are the crocketed gables and pinnacles, the open-work parapets, the delicate foliated tracery of the fourteenth-century windows. Inside is the panelling of the only stone pulpit and the lierne vaulting of the only stone roof surviving in Cheshire from the Middle Ages. The bosses of the roof are carved with scenes from the Crucifixion and the life of the Virgin. Even more remarkable is the wood carving in the gorgeous canopies of the choir stalls and in their misericords. The visitor should take care not to be in a hurry when looking at these last. He should turn up the seats one by one and savour the variety of the wood-carver's not-so-official subjects: beasts natural and fabulous, pagan mythology, medieval romance, ordinary life and its humours.

St Mary's friable sandstone and unsure foundations in land given to subsidence have necessitated constant restoration, recorded from Elizabethan times on. The greatest was that undertaken by Sir George Gilbert Scott from 1854-61. He replaced the west door and constructed above it the great window with its geometric tracery. Modern restoration is largely invisible, the pumping of 60 tons of concrete into the bases of walls and pillars.

On a three-storeyed timber building (now a shop) in the High Street is a board with the date 1584 on it. It prays God to grant the Queen a long reign

> *For She Hath Pvt Her Helping Hand*
> *To Bild This Towne Again*

In 1583 a fire, starting up in the crowded centre of the town and fanned by a strong wind, consumed the greater part of it, although the church was left unharmed. The excitement and confusion of the occasion was heightened by the presence of four bewildered bears among the fire-fighters, the bearward having released them from lock-ups threatened by the flames. Elizabeth authorised a nation-wide collection for the rebuilding and gave wood from the royal forest of Delamere. So in late Elizabethan and Jacobean times Nantwich would have looked, not an old, but a very new town.

Probably the rapid rebuilding was due as much to the efforts of the knot of wealthy gentry, whose manors lay around the town and who often had town houses in it, as it was to the benevolence of the Queen.

Webb said there were 30 or more; leading them were the lords of the manor, the Cholmondeleys, and among them well-known county families such as the Mainwarings and the Wilbrahams. They seem to have rebuilt the shops and quarters of the craftsmen in the centre of the town as densely as they were before for, until its removal in the nineteenth century, a great block of houses obscured the view of the church from the High Street. Recently another crowded area that once included the Swine and Oat Markets has made way for a shopping precinct. Nevertheless the main outline of the old streets survives, revealing how much Nantwich was a communications centre. From the main town east of the river Weaver there radiate out (from south to north) Barker Street, Pillory Street, Hospital Street and Beam Street, leading to the roads for Shrewsbury, London, Newcastle-under-Lyme, Manchester and Warrington. Across the town bridge, the Welsh Row runs out half a mile towards the village of Acton, where the road to Wrexham and North Wales divides from the road to Chester.

A number of timber-framed houses remain from Elizabethan and Jacobean times, several in the High Street and more in the Welsh Row. The outstanding house from this period was built six years before the great fire and, because it was away on the outskirts at the end of Hospital Street, survived it. It is mentioned by Webb, 'a fair timber house of Mr Randol Church, a gentleman of singular integrity', as one of the five 'gentlemanly houses' that graced the main entrances to the town. The Churche family ceased to live in it after the mid-seventeenth century and its tenants included a doctor, a tanner, a lawyer, a preacher, a cow keeper and a school-mistress who ran her school there. They altered, adapted and covered up to suit their needs and changes in the style of living but, because they were only tenants, superficially, leaving the basic structure intact underneath. In the 1930s, when it was finally put up for sale, at first no buyers from this country appeared and it seemed probable that, like several similar buildings, it would cross the Atlantic. Eventually, however, it was bought with great foresight, faith and courage by a Staffordshire doctor and his wife, who over a period of 20 years removed the accretions of three centuries. It is still in their family and is now one of the best-known restaurants in southern Cheshire, but can be visited and examined at certain hours. The house is roughly symmetrical, two gabled end-pieces linked by a hall. The hall seems still to have been used for dining and the two rooms at one end of it would, therefore, have been the kitchen and the buttery, and the single room at the other end the withdrawing room. The hall was never open to the roof, so there were at least five 'chambers' in the upper storey.

Nantwich's days as Cheshire's foremost salt town were over by the end of the seventeenth century. Yet she remained a busy and modestly thriving place, as the many fine brick eighteenth-century houses and the surprisingly sophisticated Dysart's Terrace behind St Mary's show. There were tanning, glove and shoe making; she was still an important market town and a centre for the cheese industry. Webb had said that, despite all attempts, other parts of the county and of the kingdom could 'never fully match the perfect relish of the right Nantwich cheese'. Glove and shoe making and tanning have gone and the cheese industry is much diminished, although there is a cheese factory not far from the town and a few farms still operating. But the County Agricultural College is established at Reeseheath on the outskirts of the town and it is still a stronghold for Cheshire farmers. Other light industries have come and also a considerable commuter population, some of them from adjacent Crewe but many from further afield.

Ironically enough – although Nantwich is by no means unique in this respect – it is these comparative newcomers who have pressed most strongly for a more positive attitude towards Nantwich's rich heritage from the past. The inhabitants of longer standing have been inclined to take this, if not casually, at least very much for granted. An excellent scheme has been begun for re-erecting almshouses of seventeenth- and eighteenth-century foundations, which had been allowed to decay, on a common site alongside a new welfare centre. Yet apart from this, the constant restoration work in the church and the work of isolated outsiders like the purchasers of Churche's Mansion, surprisingly little has been done to attract the tourist to Nantwich, despite all there is for him to see in it.

There is the same attitude with regard to the outstanding event in Nantwich's long history, the siege of December 1643-January 1644, when the eyes of the whole country were upon the town. The royalists had brought over some of their toughest troops from Ireland to break Parliament's hold over the north-west; the capture of Brereton's headquarters would have been a major step towards accomplishing this. The royalist commander, Lord John Byron, first tried to break the morale of townsfolk and garrison by bombarding the town with 'red-hot' shot. When this failed he attempted a dawn assault, which was bloodily repulsed. Finally he tried starvation, and this was on the point of success when a relieving force under Brereton and Sir Thomas Fairfax arrived. A battle just outside Nantwich's earth ramparts was indecisive until the garrison intervened. Although they had no knowledge of any relief arriving, they speedily organised a sally which broke into the rear of Byron's army and brought about its defeat.

For many years, even after the monarchy had been restored, the townsfolk celebrated their deliverance on 25 January by wearing holly on what was known as Holly Holy Day. The late Percy Corry, the town's local historian, tried to revive the custom. His first attempt met with little success; his second, made shortly before his death, rather more. This was, in part at any rate, because the organisation of the Sealed Knot, which specialises in refighting Civil War battles, had sprung up in the interval and provided pageantry and some re-enactment of the siege for the occasion. It is still too early to be quite sure that the custom has been re-established. Perhaps the townsfolk do not care to regard themselves as 'the descendants of Cromwell's soldiers', as one of their disgruntled parsons once called them. (In fact, the defenders of Nantwich would have been amazed to hear that they were Cromwell's soldiers. At the time of the siege Cromwell was, like Brereton, a local commander, and in a part of the country so remote from Nantwich that the majority of its defenders would never have heard of him.) Nor is Puritanism, which was probably the major factor in causing the town to support Parliament, popular now. Perhaps Holly Holy Day is best celebrated as recalling that the courage of the town's inhabitants — women as well as men, for the women had to put out fires and perform other tasks while the men guarded the walls — once won the respect of the nation.

The rest of south-east Cheshire is entirely rural; flat, well-wooded country, breaking on the Shropshire border into the hillocks and meres of the glacial moraine. There are churches of great architectural and historic interest in it and the homes of some of the most noted county families, although none are open to public inspection at the moment. A mile west of Nantwich is Acton church round which the final stages of the battle of Nantwich were fought. The church is of many periods, but the western end and the lower stages of the tower, with flat buttresses and deeply splayed lancet windows set in walls of enormous thickness, date back to the thirteenth century, when Acton was still the head manor of a great baronial fief. Inside the church are the effigies of a fourteenth-century Mainwaring and a mid-seventeenth-century Wilbraham and his wife. These were representatives of the main lines of two of the greatest families in the county.

The Wilbrahams had their residence at Woodhey, four miles west of Nantwich. Nothing remains now of their hall but a few outbuildings to a nineteenth-century farmhouse and, a field away from the farm, a little brick family chapel. Put up about 1700, it has neither altar nor communion table, but a central pulpit with the Ten Commandments on a board, oak pews down the sides and a west gallery. The gallery was, in fact, the family pew and is furnished with a fireplace at each end. A younger branch of the Wilbraham family built Dorfold Hall between Nantwich and Acton on money acquired from legal practice at the courts of Elizabeth and James I and in Ireland. The Jacobean exterior has survived almost in its entirety, and there is a good deal left of the interior also, including a plaster ceiling with pendants.

The second seat of the main branch of the Mainwarings was at Baddiley, a few miles south-west of Nantwich. Thomas Mainwaring, son of Philip the reluctant parliamentarian, whose effigy we have already noticed in Over Peover church, chose to live mostly at Baddiley. Presumably this was because it was nearer to Chester and Nantwich, for he was a notable man in county affairs under the Rump Parliament, Cromwell and Charles II. He was a J.P. throughout, sat on many commissions and acted as sheriff in 1657. His diary, now in the county archives, while excessively dry and matter-of-fact, is interesting because of the insight it gives into his attitude towards the revolutionary governments of the 1650s. This scion of one of the county's most ancient families co-operated with the upstart major-generals, carried out the Puritan fasts and observances and entertained Puritan ministers. Yet he also kept up with his numerous royalist relatives, hunted and played bowls with them and sometimes got them out of prison. On the Restoration he was not only maintained in his official position but given a baronetcy. No one protested. He had kept the framework of the old county society going in difficult times and all, except the extremists, seem to have been grateful.

The present Baddiley Hall is Georgian, built after his day, but in the little church near it he had the Creed, the Lord's Prayer, the Ten Commandments, the royal arms of Charles II (now altered to those of Victoria) and his own family arms painted on the plaster tympanum. Even apart from Sir Thomas, the church is of interest, despite its clumsy early nineteenth-century brick nave. The timber-framed chancel is very likely of medieval origin, and the wood and plaster tympanum, the only surviving one in Cheshire, would have stood behind the rood with a Doom painted upon it.

Four miles on the eastern side of Crewe is Barthomley church whose powerful square tower and battlemented aisles and clerestory make it look like a fortress. A handful of hapless villagers attempted to use it as such in December 1643. Egged on probably by the sons of their Puritan minister, they resisted Lord Byron's troops when they entered the village and were, in consequence, smoked out of the tower and butchered. It is a grim instance of the manifold non-religious purposes to which churches were put by both sides during the Civil War. Inside the church there is a richly carved camber-beam roof and a parclose screen of exquisite tracery. Once a church patronised by great county families, in particular the Fouleshursts and their successors the Crewes, now it looks from its great mound on a gaggle of little black-and-white cottages round a seventeenth-century inn. The hamlet's stillness and remoteness have survived the growth of Crewe. Whether they will also survive the intrusion of an approach road to the M6, which is barely a mile away to the east, is a different matter and one that is causing local concern.

Crewe Hall was built by Sir Randle Crewe, an important figure in English constitutional history because he lost his post as Lord Chief Justice for refusing to say that opposition to Charles I's 'forced loan' was illegal. He had already amassed sufficient wealth from his legal career, however, to put up a hall which in size and style Webb declared to be more like the mansions erected in or near London. Most of it was burnt down in 1866, but the Lord Crewe of the day got E. M. Barry to restore it so faithfully that modern experts are puzzled as to whether certain parts are Jacobean or Victorian.

Close to the Shropshire border are Doddington and Combermere Halls. Doddington was rebuilt in the eighteenth century by the first of the line of Delves Broughton, but the peel tower standing in the grounds was erected in the late Middle Ages by one of the Delves. The Jacobean figures about the tower represent Lord Audley and his four squires, whom Froissart mentions as serving the Black Prince with much distinction at the Battle of Poitiers. Modern research has shown that the family tradition that one of them was a Delves of Doddington cannot be correct; nevertheless the Delves were prominent in both the Hundred Years War and the Wars of the Roses.

Combermere is the house built by the Cottons on the ruins of the abbey, and much altered and extended in the nineteenth century. It was the home of Cheshire's greatest soldier of the Napoleonic Wars, Sir Stapleton Cotton, later Viscount Combermere, who commanded Wellington's cavalry during the Peninsular campaigns. He lived to an even greater age than his chief, with the result that his statue outside Chester castle and all the other memorials to him, which were executed after his death, give little impression of what he was like at the time of his greatest exploits. Then he was still young and, although cool, wary and reliable in action, he was also dashing, resplendent and perhaps a little vainglorious. It is said that on the most perilous of occasions he dressed in the rich uniform of the hussars and had his horse covered with gorgeous trappings. The French, who were not without experience of such characteristics among their own generals, called him *Le Lion d'Or*.

Right on the Shropshire border is the large village of Audlem, and there could hardly be a pleasanter or more interesting point of departure from Cheshire. In its centre another fortress-like church looks down from a great mound. The church's structure is peculiar but suited to its site. South aisle rises above south porch, nave above south aisle and the north aisle, resting on the flattish ground at the top of the mound, has the tower at its west end instead of at the west end of the nave. Around are many pleasant old houses, but the most interesting building of all is on lower ground to the east. It is the seventeenth-century grammar school, a tall brick house with four gables and mullioned and transomed windows. Its interest is added to by the existence in the county archives of documents relating to its erection and endowments. They provide an example of how in the troubled times of the Civil War and the Commonwealth, local feeling and goodwill could overcome divisions and difficulties.

The principal executor of the £500 endowment left by Thomas Gamull of Buerton (a nearby hall), who had become a wealthy London grocer, was his cousin Sir Francis, heart and soul of the citizen defence of Chester. Sir Francis's estate was, of course, confiscated by the Parliament and Brereton made use of the £500 to augment his war chest. After the war, however, two of the trustees, William Massie of the Moss House and William Dodd of Highfields (their black-and-white houses still stand north and south of Audlem) exerted themselves to get the endowment money repaid and released for its original purpose. As they had been parliamentarians and Massie had a war record as one of Brereton's officers, they were not prevented. A further endowment from Ralph and William Bolton of Hankelow, Merchant Taylors of London, provided for the maintenance of the schoolmaster. With local support in providing materials, the building was completed by 1655 and the school opened.

It did not achieve a particularly distinguished record. The widow and biographer of Viscount Combermere, who was one of its pupils, did not think its 'inefficient tuition' had had much to do with his future success. Its excellent endowments, however, maintained the buildings, and it lasted as a grammar school until the County Council took it over in 1910. They added to it and used it first as an elementary school and then as a secondary modern. Recently an entirely new building has been provided outside the village and the old school lies vacant. Although it has been listed, there must always be fears for the fate of an empty building and it is much to be hoped that a use can be found for it. Buildings of any kind erected during the Commonwealth are rare, school buildings rarer and school buildings with records attached almost non-existent.

There is much else of interest in and around Audlem. Although it looks so rural that industrialisation and urbanisation seem a thousand miles away, Crewe and the Potteries are, in fact, close at hand. There are now a number of commuters mixed with those whose families have lived in Audlem for many generations, and it is heartening that they have linked together in a strong amenities society, concerned that change should not be allowed to overwhelm the ancient peace and charm of the village.

ELEVEN

The Welsh Border

South of the Tarporley Gap the Cheshire highlands rise again and continue for five miles or so until they finally die out just before the south-west border of the county is reached. This is also the border with Wales; it runs west and then north for nearly 20 miles to Chester. It is a very confusing border, physically, historically and, until 1974, administratively. It is confusing physically because it often seems to ignore natural features. South of Malpas it runs four miles east of the Dee. From Shocklach to Aldford it follows the line of the river. Then it takes a sharp swing out to Dodleston which is four miles west of the Dee. Finally it comes in again to touch the suburbs of Chester. Its history is confusing because it shifted eastwards and westwards so often, particularly after the rapacious Normans had taken over from the more phlegmatic Saxons. At the time of Domesday Cheshire extended more deeply across the Dee than it has ever done since, but several times during the twelfth and thirteenth centuries, revivals brought the Welsh to the gates of Chester. When Edward I conquered Wales the administrative confusion became worse, because he did not extend the English county system to the whole of Wales, but left much of it under the control of the Lords Marcher. Their existence was not terminated until 1540 when Henry VIII made additional Welsh counties out of their lands. This explains why the bewildered traveller used to enter a little piece of Flintshire on leaving Malpas but passed into Denbighshire on crossing the Dee. He would not encounter Flintshire again unless he turned north, and even then not for many miles beyond Wrexham. The land near Malpas belonged to Welsh princes who had supported Llywelyn ap Gruffudd against Edward I, and was therefore annexed to the new county of Flint; the land beyond the Dee was granted to Marcher lords and was not included in the county system until 1540 when it formed part of Denbighshire. The local government changes have at any rate ended confusion here by lumping both into the recent creation of Clwyd.

Confusing or not, this border country is the loveliest in Cheshire. The combined Peckforton and Bickerton Hills are only a few miles in length and nowhere rise much above 700 feet. But their outline is sharp, so that from a distance they look like miniature mountains. There are steep bluffs on their western side and little wooded *cwms* creep into them. The A534 from Nantwich to Wrexham, the old salt road or *Walesmonsway* of the Middle Ages, skirts the sunny southern slope of the Peckforton Hills at Gallantry Bank, slips through the little *col* between them and the Bickerton Hills and emerges on the switchback route that runs down to the cross roads at Broxton. The lush meadows of the Dee and the panorama of the mountains of Wales are full in front. A visit to Broxton from his home in Birkenhead is said to have first awakened in Wilfred Owen that poetic feeling which later flowered so passionately in surroundings that could hardly have been more in contrast, the mud and slaughter of the western trenches in the First World War.

Off the main roads — and even they are not crowded by modern standards — all is secluded and quiet. There are no towns and no industry. The countryside is prosperous with the emphasis on pasture and dairy farming. Some of the farms still make cheese. Farms and cottages are well built; many have tall chimneys, diaper patterns in their brickwork and leaded panes. These were put up in the great rebuilding towards the end of the last century undertaken by or under the influence of the Tollemaches of Peckforton, who were paternalistic improving landlords. Yet rural depopulation and modern farming methods have made the landscape uncannily empty. You can travel the good by-roads and meet only the occasional car, more rarely the cyclist and hardly ever anyone on foot. There is activity in the farmyards but never much in the fields. Sometimes there are herds of cattle; sometimes the only animals visible are horses and these are not for farming purposes.

On the great sandstone outcrop just north of the Peckforton Hills stand the remains of Beeston castle. The visitor is apt to be confused by the appearance of a second castle on the end of the Peckforton ridge opposite, which seems more substantial and from many angles just as convincingly medieval. This is Peckforton 'Castle', until recently the main seat of the Tollemache family and designed for the first Lord Tollemache by Salvin in 1844. Unlike Cholmondeley 'Castle' and others, Peckforton is not just a façade of turrets and battlements covering an assembly of conventional early nineteenth-century rooms. It has inner and outer wards with real gatehouses, a real (though waterless) moat and a great hall, open to the roof, with a screens passage at one end and a raised dais at the other. It deserves the title which Gilbert Scott gave it of, 'the very height of masquerading'. The present turreted entrance to Beeston Castle and the wall on both sides of it are also Tollemache work.

Beeston's real outer ward is halfway up the eastern and gentlest slope of the crag. Webb, however, said it was difficult to keep one's footing on any part of the hill and modern visitors will not be inclined to dispute his statement. It must have been a nightmare getting any wheeled transport up to the main gate of the castle in wet weather. The outer gatehouse is now no more than a great gap in the curtain wall of the ward; it was probably destroyed in the 'slighting' after the Civil War.

What is left of Beeston Castle is very ruinous but sufficient to make plain its extraordinary layout. Only the central part of the outer curtain wall, which runs along an escarpment halfway up the slope, survives, and it never completely encircled the hill because the north-western side is sheer precipice. Nevertheless it must have been about 2,000 feet in length and the ward which it encloses is enormous. By contrast the inner ward at the summit of the hill, which is separated from the outer ward by a rock-cut ditch and protected on all other sides by precipices, is tiny. Its gatehouse and two further semi-circular towers fronting the ditch survive, but the remainder of the wall of the inner ward has never had any towers on it, for it stands on the very edge of the precipice. The strength which nature gave to the site was completed by the presence of water and deep wells were dug in both wards. The shaft to the upper well and its parapet still exist.

We know that the castle was built by Ranulf III, Earl of Chester, in the 1220s and altered and strengthened 50 years later by Edward I during the Welsh Wars. It never stood a siege during the Middle Ages and this was not simply because of its impregnability. It was the product of unusual circumstances which passed away shortly after it was built. In a way it is the supreme monument to Cheshire's semi-independent position under the Norman earls which has been referred to in the Introduction. Ranulf III, the most influential of the Norman earls, was loyal to King John when most of the rest of the barons were not, and played a major part in saving the throne for John's infant son, Henry III. But he did not get on well with those who ran the country during the new king's minority. In addition he had growing up beside him the power of the Welsh prince, Llywelyn the Great of Gwynedd. About the time that he built Beeston, Ranulf married his nephew and heir, John the Scot, to Llywelyn's daughter, Helen. Beeston is better placed to hinder an invasion from England through the Tarporley Gap than it is one from North Wales, and it looks very much as if it was intended to face both ways, to be part of a triangular relationship between Cheshire, England and Gwynedd.

Shortly after it was built, Ranulf and his nephew died and Henry III took over Cheshire, making his son Edward its earl. Yet there was a brief moment during the Barons' War of 1264-5 when it looked as if the castle might fulfil its original role. Simon de Montfort, the baronial leader, when he gained control of the country, took over the earldom of Chester and put a garrison into Beeston. He was in firm alliance with Llywelyn ap Gruffudd, the new prince of Gwynedd. When Prince Edward finally overthrew Simon at the battle of Evesham, the Montfortians in the strongholds of Chester and Beeston, feeling that Llywelyn would back them, contemplated resistance. But, with their leader dead and most of the barons going over to Edward, they changed their minds and surrendered.

After this Beeston remained firmly in royal hands but, once the great Snowdonian castles had been built, it was very much a second, or even a third, line of defence against trouble in Wales. By Tudor times it was deserted and ruinous and Webb reported 'tourists' throwing stones down the wells to guess their depths.

Then came the Civil War and the military role Beeston had hitherto been denied. Brereton garrisoned it, intending it chiefly as a safe storehouse for arms, provisions and the property of his supporters. This being so, he chose as governor one 'Captain' Steele, a peacetime cheese factor who was also a 'godly professor', i.e. Puritan, and therefore not likely to betray the cause. He had, however, no military experience, nor, as it proved, the courage to face an emergency. This arose when Lord Byron, about to move against Nantwich and unable to spare the men to besiege Beeston, sent a daring officer, one Captain Sandford, and eight musketeers to attempt a surprise. The clumsily equipped musketeers can hardly have scaled the precipices and, as all other routes led to the outer ward, they must have zig-zagged up the north slope to the wall of the inner ward, where an accomplice in the garrison probably helped them to get in. Steele, in the outer ward, had 60 soldiers to Sandford's eight. Nevertheless he tamely surrendered the fortress and was allowed to march his garrison off to Nantwich with 'the honours of war'. The Nantwich Council of War, not thinking there was much 'honour' in his action, threw him into prison and later had him shot. At his final confession he denied treachery, but was very worried about an illicit love affair he had been having with a maid in one of the inns he frequented when carrying out his peace-time profession. He had paid very dearly for his 'godly professings' and the position these had got him into.

This was the end of Beeston as a fortress. In the nineteenth century, when the Tollemaches acquired it as part of the estates of the Wilbrahams of Woodhey, it was thrown open to the public and made the scene of festivities on special occasions. Sports were held and bands played (somewhat precariously one would have thought) in the outer ward. From the inner ward rockets were launched and cannon fired. Either this part of the castle was a good deal less ruinous then or the Tollemache administration had stronger nerves than their successors, the Ministry of Works, who have closed it to the public altogether now.

Almost under the shadow of Beeston is the large village of Bunbury. It is really three villages conjoined: the old Churchtown round the medieval church; Lower Bunbury which grew in Tudor times beside enclosures from the townfields; Bunbury Heath which sprang from nineteenth-century enclosure of the open common. The commuter has now discovered but not spoilt Bunbury; everywhere there are charming groups of eighteenth- and nineteenth-century houses, ranging from cottages to villas.

Bunbury's chief glory is its great church. Like so many of Cheshire's finest churches, it was completely rebuilt in the fourteenth century and then altered and added to in the early sixteenth century. The chancel and its east window, which has flowing curvilinear tracery rare in Cheshire, and the lower stages of the tower, date from the first period; the upper stages of the tower, the battlements and pinnacles, the large aisle windows and the Ridley chapel with its stone screen from the second. The inevitable Victorian restoration destroyed the old pewing, some of the screens and some frescoes which had recently been uncovered. But it did provide the church with a proper clerestory which it had never had before. In 1940 a German land mine, dropping near the north-east corner, caused a totally unlooked-for twentieth-century restoration. This took 14 years to complete but has given the church an atmosphere of lightness and spaciousness. Clearer modern glass replaces some very heavy Victorian work which was destroyed, and there is a new roof.

In the chancel lies the alabaster effigy of Sir Hugh Calveley, builder of the fourteenth-century church. The marvellous and well-preserved reproduction of the arms and armour of the day make it Cheshire's finest medieval tomb. In origin a minor squire, Sir Hugh won fame and fortune as a companion-in-arms of the Black Prince. He rose to become deputy governor of Calais, governor of Brest, admiral of England. Some have seen in him the pattern of chivalry. It seems more likely, however, that he was a formidable and efficient professional soldier – Froissart has a story of his accepting with great reluctance the command of the reserve and then winning the subsequent battle by bringing this in at precisely the right moment – but morally neither better nor worse than most of his kind. At any rate in his later years he tried to set his account right with his Creator, not only by rebuilding Bunbury church, but by re-endowing it to be served by a 'college' of six priests.

Also in the chancel is the effigy of Sir George Beeston, with ruff and trunks protruding from his suit of black armour. His life, which spanned the entire sixteenth-century, appears unbelievable but is well documented. Born in 1499, he fought in France under Henry VIII, in Scotland in the reign of Edward VI and in 1588, when he was 89, commanded the *Dreadnought* against the Armada. Elizabeth, with good reason, gave him a knighthood for this feat. Two years before his death in 1601, when he must have been 100 or very near it, he was vigorously quarrelling with the 'preacher' of Bunbury about the position of the pulpit.

Bunbury in the early seventeenth century must have been in a ferment of religious unorthodoxy. The 'preacher' with whom Sir George quarrelled was not the incumbent, but existed as the result of an endowment left by Thomas Aldersey, a member of a local family of small squires, who had become a wealthy London haberdasher. Good preaching was an essential of the Puritan movement and, as the parish incumbents were sometimes incapable of providing it, Puritan squires and merchants often put up money for an additional 'preacher' in a particular area. As a result of the Aldersey endowment, Bunbury had a succession of able and zealous 'preachers', some of whom gained national fame. Yet at the same time the records reveal that Bunbury had more avowed adherents of the old faith than any other parish in Cheshire except Malpas. These Roman Catholics ranged from members of the local squirearchy, even including the Alderseys, to tailors, glovers, tenant farmers and farm labourers.

This refusal in the parish to accept the orthodox Anglican service as all-sufficient continued into the next century. The church contains behind a grille a copy of Birkett's *Commentary on the New Testament.* This was presented by the bishop of Chester to a group which had been formed in the parish to study the scriptures, originally with the approval of the vicar and the local squire, Richard Davenport of Calveley. In 1749, however, its leader, Richard Cawley of Moat Farm, Alpraham, invited John Wesley to visit the group. He came and then and on subsequent occasions preached at Moat Farm. Although the squire remained friendly, inviting Wesley to dinner and refusing to countenance any rabbling of Methodists, the vicar grew cool and the society ceased to meet in the church.

The claim that this group and Wesley's visit to it began Methodism in Cheshire cannot be upheld, however. There were many other such groups: in Northwich, Mobberley, Adlington and Millington, near Stockport, Macclesfield and Congleton. Some of these, and others all over the country, were quite as old as Bunbury's. They were a symptom of a widespread craving for something more moving and fundamental than was provided then by the regular forms of worship, Anglican or Nonconformist. Wesley did not inaugurate them; he encouraged them and then fused them into a great national movement.

Malpas, at the further end of the southern highlands, is smaller than Bunbury but more compact. It, too, has a great medieval church, high on a mound above the village. In the post-Conquest period Malpas was the *caput* or head manor of one of the largest baronies in Cheshire. It commanded an important road south down the Welsh border and had a castle, whose 'motte' is still visible as a green mound behind the church. At the end of the Middle Ages a junior branch of the great Brereton family settled there. Sir Randle Brereton served Henry VII and VIII in military posts of importance at home and abroad. He became chamberlain of Chester, the earl's principal deputy in the county. He had his hall at the end of the village street and founded a school and almshouses as well. His line did not long survive him, however, and all his buildings fell into decay and disappeared. School and almhouses were revived by the neighbouring Cholmondeleys in the eighteenth century and their pedimented and pilastered buildings survive.

The church of Malpas is yet another example of a fourteenth-century rebuilding with late fifteenth- and early sixteenth-century additions and alterations. In this case the later work is dominant. Outside are the wide Perpendicular windows of aisles and clerestory, the pinnacles and embattled parapets. Inside are the wooden screens of the Brereton and Cholmondeley chapels, the alabaster effigies of Sir Randle Brereton and his wife and an Elizabethan Cholmondeley and his wife, and yet another magnificent camber-beam roof.

West of Malpas the border with Wales turns north and along it, at Shocklach, Aldford, Pulford and Dodleston, are more remains of the primitive 'motte-and-bailey' castles of the post-Conquest era. The most clearly visible 'mottes', with some remains of the ramparts of the baileys, are near the nineteenth-century churches of Aldford and Pulford. They were intended mainly as a defence against the Welsh and there were elaborate arrangements for contingents from eastern Cheshire to help to man them in time of danger. Though how, with the poor communications of those days and the suddenness of Welsh raids, these ever got there in time remains a mystery.

Shocklach church, for reasons unknown, is a mile from the site of the castle and stands quite alone, as the present village has grown up elsewhere. With not much growth of population since early medieval times, the Norman nave with its crude but attractive south doorway and the little fourteenth-century chancel have been allowed to remain. The interior fittings – plaster ceiling, font, pulpit and communion rail – date from the seventeenth and eighteenth centuries, but match the simplicity of the original structure.

Three miles further north, where the Dee meanders in intricate curves through its flood plain, is the only other surviving medieval bridge in Cheshire besides Chester bridge. Its nine stone arches link the Cheshire village of Farndon with the Welsh village of Holt, and almost the only noticeable relic of ancient racial strive is the insistence of those on the Welsh side that it is *Holt* bridge and those on the Cheshire side that it is *Farndon* bridge. It was built in the fourteenth century, presumably to speed the flow of traffic along the Walesmonsway now that this had been increased by the end of the wars against the Welsh. Today it is undoubtedly a hindrance to the flow of modern traffic – lights have had to be placed on it – but one justified by the extra distinction that it confers on an already beautiful landscape. Richard Wilson thought it worthy of an oil painting, now in the National Gallery.

As the Dee at this point was the dividing line between parliamentarian Cheshire and royalist North Wales, the bridge was the scene of a good deal of fighting during the Civil War. This was the reason for the little guard house in the middle of the bridge, shown on Wilson's painting but removed soon afterwards. Farndon church, which the parliamentarians apparently used as a strong point, had to be largely rebuilt afterwards, and in it was placed a stained-glass window which is apparently the only one in existence with a Civil War theme. It commemorates the royalist defenders of Chester and was set up by the local squire, William Barnston of Churton, who commanded a company in the defence. The officers, who can be distinguished by the coats-of-arms placed alongside them, are, in the top row, Sir Richard Grosvenor, Sir William Mainwaring and Barnston himself, in the centre, standing outside his tent, Sir Francis Gamull, commander of the citizen guard and deputy governor, and in the bottom row the standard bearer, Sir William Berrington. The other figures are those of musketeers, pikemen, halberdiers and drummers, while the central panels are filled with arms and accoutrements. It is a most comprehensive delineation of Civil War costume and equipment.

Aldford to Eccleston is the heart of the Grosvenor country and in the centre of it is Eaton Hall. Even if the claim of the Grosvenors to trace their ancestry back to the Conquest is dubious, they were certainly well established in the county by the fourteenth century, when they appeared on the national scene as contestants in the first known dispute concerning the right to a coat-of-arms. On an expedition to Scotland Sir Robert

Grosvenor was found to have the same arms — *azure a bend or* — as Sir Richard Scrope, one of King Richard II's important household officials. With all the great ones of the land against him in the enquiry that followed as to which of the knights had a prior claim to the arms, Grosvenor was forced to abandon them and select others. That the decision continued to rankle throughout 500 years was shown by the first Duke of Westminster choosing *Bend Or* for the name of the most famous of his many famous race horses.

By the seventeenth century the Grosvenors were among the leaders of the county squirearchy. The Sir Richard Grosvenor of Charles I's days was the first Cheshire man to distinguish himself as an M.P. (Cheshire sent no representatives to Parliament until 1547.) Although afterwards a royalist, he was one of the strongest opponents of the king's high church policy in the Commons. It was his grandson, Sir Thomas Grosvenor, who laid the foundation of the much greater wealth and position which the family came to enjoy. Seeking to bolster up the family fortunes with city wealth, as many other county families were doing, in 1677 he married Mary Davies, heiress to a London financier who had purchased the manor of Ebury. The manor contained the land into which London's West End expanded in the eighteenth and nineteenth centuries. Belgravia takes it name from Belgrave, still no more than a hamlet on the Eaton estate, and in Belgravia are names such as Eaton Square, Grosvenor Place, Chester Row and Eccleston Square. With their new wealth the Grosvenors became part of the national establishment. After a brief flirtation with Jacobitism they became solidly Whig and remained so as long as the Whig party lasted. The land they purchased in Chester and the money they poured into it ensured them or their nominees the town's two seats in Parliament. In 1761 the head of the house became a peer, in 1831 Marquis of Westminster, in 1874 Duke.

Their family homes have kept pace with their advancement. Sir Thomas pulled down the old timber hall and had William Samwell design him a brick mansion of classical symmetry. The first Marquis got William Porden to transform this into a stone mansion with early Gothic Revival pinnacles, battlements and iron tracery. The first Duke then employed Alfred Waterhouse, the architect of Manchester Town Hall, to alter and enlarge Porden's house out of all recognition. It became a vast *château* to which the Rhine or the Loire would have been a more fitting foreground than the Dee. Although the Duke remarked that, if he were his own heir, he would pull it down and start afresh, Waterhouse's Eaton Hall lasted until after the Second World War. Then deterioration caused by military occupation and the impossibility of ever gathering together again the army of servants required to maintain it, caused it to be demolished. The concrete structure that has just risen at Eaton, while much more modest in size, demonstrates that the present Duke, like his ancestors, believes in building a home in accordance with the advanced architectural ideas of his own day.

At least it must be said of the Grosvenors that their wealth and position have never made them forsake the dwelling place of their forbears nor the welfare of its community. The first Duke not only rebuilt Eaton Hall but the churches of Aldford and Eccleston and all the farms and cottages on the estate, and did not let the agricultural depression of the late nineteenth-century halt the good work. While he employed Waterhouse for Eaton Hall and Bodley for the church at Eccleston, the greater part of the estate buildings were designed by the Cheshire architect, John Douglas. Fortunately he was an architect of great professional skill and sensibility. He put up farmhouses which were dignified but workable, cottages which were aesthetic yet hygienic.

North of Eccleston the Dee passes Heron Bridge, where the Romans had an industrial site and a staging post for the river traffic to their tile factory at Holt, and then sweeps round the curve of the Earl's Eye into Chester. So we end where we began, with the city round whose strength and ancient fame the county of Cheshire was first formed and which, despite all changes, is still the seat of its administration and the most noteworthy place in it.

Index